HAMLET

William Shakespeare

Prestwick House
LITERARY TOUCHSTONE CLASSICS™
P.O. Box 658 Clayton, Delaware 19938 • www.prestwickhouse.com

SENIOR EDITOR: Paul Moliken

EDITORS: Elizabeth Osborne, Lisa M. Miller, Sarah Enloe, Sarah Ann Ill, Bob Jones, and Anna Gonzales

COVER DESIGN: Maria J. Mendoza

PRODUCTION: Jeremy Clark

COSTUME: Provided by Actor's Attic • www.actorsattic.com

Prestwick House

LITERARY TOUCHSTONE CLASSICS ½

P.O. BOX 658 • CLAYTON, DELAWARE 19938

TEL: 1.800.932.4593

FAX: 1.888.718.9333

WEB: www.prestwickhouse.com

Prestwick House Teaching Units™, *Activity Packs*™, and *Response Journals*™ are the perfect complement for these editions. To purchase teaching resources for this book, visit www.prestwickhouse.com

ISBN   978-1-58049-591-2

CONTENTS

STRATEGIES FOR UNDERSTANDING SHAKESPEARE'S LANGUAGE 4

READING POINTERS FOR SHARPER INSIGHTS 10

DRAMATIS PERSONAE 13

ACT I
    SCENE 1 15
    SCENE 2 20
    SCENE 3 27
    SCENE 4 31
    SCENE 5 34

ACT II
    SCENE 1 41
    SCENE 2 45

ACT III
    SCENE 1 61
    SCENE 2 66
    SCENE 3 77
    SCENE 4 80

ACT IV
    SCENE 1 87
    SCENE 2 88
    SCENE 3 89
    SCENE 4 92
    SCENE 5 94
    SCENE 6 101
    SCENE 7 102

ACT V
    SCENE 1 109
    SCENE 2 117

VOCABULARY AND GLOSSARY 129

Strategies for Understanding Shakespeare's Language

1. **When reading verse, note the appropriate phrasing and intonation.**

   DO NOT PAUSE AT THE END OF A LINE unless there is a mark of punctuation. Shakespearean verse has a rhythm of its own, and once a reader gets used to it, the rhythm becomes very natural to speak in and read. Beginning readers often find it helpful to read a short pause at a comma and a long pause for a period, colon, semicolon, dash, or question mark.

   Here's an example from *The Merchant of Venice*, Act IV, Scene i:

   > The quality of mercy is not strain'd, *(short pause)*
   > It droppeth as the gentle rain from heaven
   > Upon the place beneath: *(long pause)* it is twice blest; *(long pause)*
   > It blesseth him that gives, *(short pause)* and him that takes; *(long pause)*
   > 'Tis mightiest in the mighties; *(long pause)* it becomes
   > The throned monarch better than his crown; *(long pause)*

2. **Read from punctuation mark to punctuation mark for meaning.**

   In addition to helping you read aloud, punctuation marks define units of thought. Try to understand each unit as you read, keeping in mind that periods, colons, semicolons, and question marks signal the end of a thought. Here's an example from *The Taming of the Shrew*: Act I, Scene i:

   > Luc. Tranio, I saw her coral lips to move,
   >   And with her breath she did perfume the air;
   >   Sacred, and sweet, was all I saw in her.
   > Tra. Nay, then, 'tis time to stir him from his
   >   trance.
   >   I pray, awake, sir: if you love the maid,
   >   Bend thoughts and wits to achieve her.

The first unit of thought is from "Tranio" to "air":
He saw her lips move, and her breath perfumed the air.

The second thought ("Sacred, and sweet...") re-emphasizes the first.

Tranio replies that Lucentio needs to awaken from his trance and try to win "the maid." These two sentences can be considered one unit of thought.

3. In an **inverted sentence**, the verb comes before the subject. Some lines will be easier to understand if you put the subject first and reword the sentence. For example, look at the line below:

    "Never was seen so black a day as this:" (*Romeo and Juliet*, Act IV, Scene v)

    You can change its inverted pattern so it is more easily understood:

    "A day as black as this was never seen:"

4. An **ellipsis** occurs when a word or phrase is left out. In *Romeo and Juliet*, Benvolio asks Romeo's father and mother if they know the problem that is bothering their son. Romeo's father answers:

    "I neither know it nor can learn of him" (*Romeo and Juliet*, Act I, Scene i).

    This sentence can easily be understood to mean,

    *"I neither know [the cause of] it,
    nor can [I] learn [about it from] him."*

5. As you read longer speeches, keep track of the subject, verb, and object— *who* did *what* to *whom*.

    In the clauses below, note the subject, verbs, and objects:

    Ross: The king hath happily received, Macbeth,
        The news of thy success: and when he reads
        Thy personal venture in the rebel's fight... (*Macbeth*, Act I, Scene iii)

    1ˢᵗ clause: *The king hath happily received, Macbeth,/The news of thy success:*
    SUBJECT – The king
    VERB – has received
    OBJECT – the news [of Macbeth's success]

2nd clause: *and when he reads/thy personal venture in the rebel's fight,*
SUBJECT – he [the king]
VERB – reads
OBJECT – [about] your venture

In addition to following the subject, verb, and object of a clause, you also need to track pronoun references. In the following soliloquy, Romeo, who is madly in love with Juliet, secretly observes her as she steps out on her balcony. To help you keep track of the pronoun references, we've made margin notes. (Note that the feminine pronoun sometimes refers to Juliet, but sometimes does not.)

But, soft! what light through yonder window breaks?
It is the east, and Juliet is the sun!
Arise, fair sun, and kill the envious moon,
Who* is already sick and pale with grief,   *"Who" refers to the moon.*
That thou her* maid* art more fair than she:*   *"thou her maid" refers*
                                                                                     to Juliet, the sun.
                                                                 "she" and "her" refer to the moon.

In tracking the line of action in a passage, it is useful to identify the main thoughts that are being expressed and paraphrase them. Note the following passage in which Hamlet expresses his feelings about the death of his father and the remarriage of his mother:

O God! a beast that wants discourse of reason
Would have mourn'd longer—married with my uncle,
My father's brother, but no more like my father
Than I to Hercules. (*Hamlet*, Act I, Scene ii)

Paraphrasing the three main points, we find that Hamlet is saying:

- a mindless beast would have mourned the death of its mate longer than my mother did
- she married my uncle, my father's brother
- my uncle is not at all like my father

If you are having trouble understanding Shakespeare, the first rule is to read it out loud, just as an actor rehearsing would have to do. That will help you understand how one thought is connected to another.

6. Shakespeare frequently uses **metaphor** to illustrate an idea in a unique way. Pay careful attention to the two dissimilar objects or ideas being compared. In *Macbeth*, Duncan, the king says:

I have begun to plant thee, and will labour
To make thee full of growing. (*Macbeth*, Act I, Scene v)

The king compares Macbeth to a tree he can plant and watch grow.

7. An **allusion** is a reference to some event, person, place, or artistic work, not directly explained or discussed by the writer; it relies on the reader's familiarity with the item referred to. Allusion is a quick way of conveying information or presenting an image. In the following lines, Romeo alludes to Diana, goddess of the hunt and of chastity, and to Cupid's arrow (love).

> ROMEO: Well, in that hit you miss: she'll not be hit
> with Cupid's arrow, she hath Dian's wit;
> and in strong proof of chastity well arm'd
> (*Romeo and Juliet*, Act I, Scene i)

8. Contracted words are words in which a letter has been left out. Some that frequently appear:

be't	on't	wi'
do't	t'	'sblood
'gainst	ta'en	i'
'tis	e'en	
'bout	know'st	'twill
ne'er	o'	o'er

9. Archaic, obsolete, and familiar words with unfamiliar definitions may also cause problems.

- **Archaic Words:** Some archaic words, like *thee, thou, thy,* and *thine,* are instantly understandable, while others, like *betwixt,* cause a momentary pause.

- **Obsolete Words:** If it were not for the notes in a Shakespeare text, obsolete words could be a problem; words like *beteem* are usually not found in student dictionaries. In these situations, however, a quick glance at the book's notes will solve the problem.

- **Familiar Words with Unfamiliar Definitions:** Another problem is those familiar words whose definitions have changed. Because readers think they know the word, they do not check the notes. For example, in this comment from *Much Ado About Nothing,* Act I, Scene i, the word *an* means "if":

BEATRICE: Scratching could not make it worse, *an* 'twere such
a face as yours were.

For this kind of word, we have included margin notes.

10. **Wordplay—puns, double entendres, and malapropisms:**

- A **pun** is a literary device that achieves humor or emphasis by playing on ambiguities. Two distinct meanings are suggested either by the same word or by two similar-sounding words.

- A **double entendre** is a kind of pun in which a word or phrase has a second, usually sexual, meaning.

- A **malapropism** occurs when a character mistakenly uses a word that he or she has confused with another word. In *Romeo and Juliet,* the Nurse tells Romeo that she needs to have a "confidence" with him, when she should have said "conference." Mockingly, Benvolio then says she probably will "indite" (rather than "invite") Romeo to dinner.

11. **Shakespeare's Language:**

Our final word on Shakespeare's language is adapted by special permission from Ralph Alan Cohen's book *Shakesfear and How to Cure It—A Guide to Teaching Shakespeare.*

What's so hard about Shakespeare's language? Many students come to Shakespeare's language assuming that the language of his period is substantially different from ours. In fact, 98% of the words in Shakespeare are current-usage English words. So why does it sometimes seem hard to read Shakespeare? There are three main reasons:

- Originally, Shakespeare wrote the words for an actor to illustrate them as he spoke. In short, the play you have at hand was meant for the stage, not for the page.

- Shakespeare had the same love of reforming and rearranging words in such places as hip-hop and sportscasting today. His plays reflect an excitement about language and an inventiveness that becomes enjoyable once the reader gets into the spirit of it.

- Since Shakespeare puts all types of people on stage, those characters will include some who are pompous, some who are devious, some who are boring, and some who are crazy, and all of these will speak in ways that are sometimes trying. Modern playwrights creating similar characters have them speak in similarly challenging ways.

12. **Stage Directions:**

Shakespeare's stagecraft went hand-in-hand with his wordcraft. For that reason, we believe it is important for the reader to know which stage directions are modern and which derive from Shakespeare's earliest text—the single-play Quartos or the Folio, the first collected works (1623). All stage directions appear in italics, but the brackets enclose modern additions to the stage directions. Readers may assume that the unbracketed stage directions appear in the Quarto and/or Folio versions of the play.

13. **Scene Locations:**

Shakespeare imagined his plays, first and foremost, on the stage of his outdoor or indoor theatre. The original printed versions of the plays do not give imaginary scene locations, except when they are occasionally mentioned in the dialogue. As an aid to the reader, this edition *does* include scene locations at the beginning of each scene, but puts all such locations in brackets to remind the reader that *this is not what Shakespeare envisioned and only possibly what he imagined.*

Reading Pointers for Sharper Insights

As you read *Hamlet*, be aware of the following themes and concepts:

Death: *Hamlet* begins shortly after the murder of a king and ends with the deaths of four of the major characters. Throughout the play, at least four others die, either onstage or off. Hamlet considers what death is many times during the play. He wonders about suicide, the afterlife, and what happens to the physical body after death. The scene with the gravediggers, while filled with humor, shows Hamlet's preoccupation with death. And even later in Act V, Hamlet states that being ready for death is what is important.

Sickness and imbalance: In the play, not only are many characters out of balance, but the whole country of Denmark, with Claudius at its head, seems to have grown ill. Natural order has been disrupted, which manifests itself through the duplicity of the court, the turning of friends into foes, the rejection of love, the appearance of the Ghost, Hamlet's condemnations of women, and the continued use of lies and deception for personal gain. One can assume that under the rule of King Hamlet, these symptoms of corruption were infrequent.

Madness: It is sometimes difficult to determine who is sane in the play. At one time, Hamlet claims he will merely pretend to be mad; at another, he claims that he cannot reason properly and that his mind is diseased. His mother, Polonius, and Ophelia all believe he is insane, but his friend Horatio does not. Polonius is not mad, but is so intently and illogically focused on Hamlet's behavior that he could be said to be obsessive to the point of lunacy. Ophelia is driven mad by the murder of her father, among other factors, and commits suicide.

Acting and plays: Notice the references to the differences between being on a stage and actually living. This type of duality runs throughout *Hamlet*. Except for Horatio, few characters in *Hamlet* consistently say what they believe is true. Claudius, who hates and fears Hamlet, pretends to love him; Ophelia must deny Hamlet her love, while Hamlet claims never to have loved; Rosencrantz and Guildenstern act like friends, but they are really spies; and Hamlet is not really sure if the Ghost is playing a part to send him to hell. The play-within-a-play—actors performing a scene written by Hamlet, pretending to portray a real event—is a crucial element in Hamlet's decision-making.

Children and parents: There are two family relationships in the play. Hamlet's is the most difficult, and he makes sure that everyone at court understands how it pains him. Claudius, who killed King Hamlet, was his uncle, but is now his father, which makes Hamlet both a nephew and a son to the same man. Gertrude, once a sister-in-law to Claudius, is now his wife. Polonius wants his son Laertes to be independent and mature, but sends a servant to spy on him. Ophelia obviously loves Hamlet, yet out of duty, obeys Polonius and rejects him.

Sleep and dreams: Hamlet is consumed by the need for revenge, yet he seems to be incapable of taking any action to obtain it. Instead, he only debates what he should do, contemplates whether the Ghost tells the truth, wonders if suicide is preferable to regicide, intellectualizes his possibilities, and frequently doubts his choices; yet he constantly berates his inaction. Until Hamlet's inadvertent killing of Polonius, he has taken no action on the Ghost's demand.

Symbols and motifs: rot/decay; gardens/flowers/weeds; worms/snakes/venom/poison; eyes/ears/skulls; incest/sexuality; black/darkness; morality/corruption; appearances/reality/dreams

HAMLET

WILLIAM SHAKESPEARE

DRAMATIS PERSONAE

CLAUDIUS, King of Denmark
GERTRUDE, Queen of Denmark, mother of Hamlet
Ghost of Hamlet's Father
HAMLET, son to the late King, and nephew to [Claudius] the present King
OPHELIA, daughter of Polonius
HORATIO, friend of Hamlet
POLONIUS, Lord Chamberlain, advisor to Claudius
LAERTES, son of Polonius
VOLTIMAND, courtier
CORNELIUS, courtier
ROSENCRANTZ, courtier
GUILDENSTERN, courtier
OSRIC, courtier
A Gentleman, courtier
A Priest
MARCELLUS, an officer
BERNARDO, an officer
FRANCISCO, a soldier
REYNALDO, servant to Polonius
FORTINBRAS, Prince of Norway
Players
Two Clowns, gravediggers
A Norwegian Captain
English Ambassadors
Lords, Ladies, Officers, Soldiers, Sailors, Messengers, Attendants

HAMLET

[ACT I]

Horatio in english
means the voice
of reason

[SCENE I]

[Elsinore. A platform before the Castle.]

Enter Bernardo and Francisco, two Sentinels

BERNARDO: Who's there?
FRANCISCO: Nay, answer me. Stand and unfold¹ yourself.   ¹*reveal*
BERNARDO: Long live the King!
FRANCISCO: Bernardo?
5 BERNARDO: He.
FRANCISCO: You come most carefully upon your hour.
BERNARDO: 'Tis now struck twelve. Get thee to bed, Francisco.
FRANCISCO: For this relief much thanks. 'Tis bitter cold,
    And I am sick at heart.
10 BERNARDO: Have you had quiet guard?
FRANCISCO: Not a mouse stirring.
BERNARDO: Well, good night.
    If you do meet Horatio and Marcellus,
    The rivals² of my watch, bid them make haste.   ²*replacements*
15 FRANCISCO: I think I hear them. Stand, ho! Who is there?

Enter Horatio and Marcellus.

HORATIO: Friends to this ground.
MARCELLUS: And liegemen³ to the Dane.   ³*loyal followers*
FRANCISCO: Give you good night.
MARCELLUS: O, farewell, honest soldier.
20   Who hath relieved you?
FRANCISCO: Bernardo hath my place.
    Give you good night.   *Exit Francisco.*
MARCELLUS: Holla, Bernardo!

BERNARDO: Say,
25   What, is Horatio there?
HORATIO: A piece of him.
BERNARDO: Welcome, Horatio. Welcome, good Marcellus.
MARCELLUS: What, has this thing appear'd again to-night?
BERNARDO: I have seen nothing.
30 MARCELLUS: Horatio says 'tis but our fantasy,
        And will not let belief take hold of him
        Touching this dreaded sight, twice seen of us.
        Therefore I have entreated him along
        With us to watch the minutes of this night,
35   That if again this apparition come
        He may approve⁴ our eyes and speak to it.
HORATIO: Tush,⁵ tush, 'twill not appear.
BERNARDO: Sit down awhile,
        And let us once again assail your ears,
40   That are so fortified against our story,
        What we two nights have seen.
HORATIO: Well, sit we down,
        And let us hear Bernardo speak of this.
BERNARDO: Last night of all,
45   When yond same star⁶ that's westward from the pole
        Had made his course to illume that part of heaven
        Where now it burns, Marcellus and myself,
        The bell⁷ then beating one—

Enter the Ghost.

MARCELLUS: Peace! break thee off! Look where it comes
50   again!
BERNARDO: In the same figure, like the King that's dead.
MARCELLUS: Thou art a scholar; speak to it, Horatio.
BERNARDO: Looks it not like the King? Mark it, Horatio.
HORATIO: Most like. It harrows me with fear and wonder.
55 BERNARDO: It would be spoke to.
MARCELLUS: Question it, Horatio.
HORATIO: What art thou that usurp'st⁸ this time of night,
        Together with that fair and warlike form
        In which the majesty of buried Denmark
60   Did sometimes march? By heaven I charge thee, speak!

⁴*prove correct*

⁵*a term indicating scorn*

⁶*North Star*

⁷*clock*

⁸*wrongfully seize*

MARCELLUS: It is offended.

BERNARDO: See, it stalks away!

HORATIO: Stay! speak, speak! I charge thee, speak!

Exit the Ghost.

MARCELLUS: 'Tis gone, and will not answer.

65 BERNARDO: How now, Horatio? You tremble and look pale.

Is not this something more than fantasy?

What think you on't?

HORATIO: Before my God, I might not this believe

Without the sensible and true avouch[9]   [9]*assurance*

70 Of mine own eyes.

MARCELLUS: Is it not like the King?

HORATIO: As thou art to thyself.

Such was the very armour he had on

When he the ambitious Norway combated.

75 So frown'd he once when, in an angry parle,[10]   [10]*discussion*

He smote[11] the sledded Polacks on the ice.   [11]*struck down*

'Tis strange.

MARCELLUS: Thus twice before, and jump[12] at this dead hour,   [12]*exactly*

With martial stalk[13] hath he gone by our watch.   [13]*stride*

80 HORATIO: In what particular thought to work I know not;

But, in the gross and scope[14] of my opinion,   [14]*general range*

This bodes some strange eruption[15] to our state.   [15]*disturbance*

MARCELLUS: Good now, sit down, and tell me, he that knows,

Why this same strict and most observant watch

85 So nightly toils[16] the subject[17] of the land,   [16]*puts to work*   [17]*common people*

And why such daily cast of brazen[18] cannon,   [18]*brass*

And foreign mart for implements of war,

Why such impress[19] of shipwrights, whose sore[20] task   [19]*forced service*   [20]*difficult*

Does not divide the Sunday from the week.

90 What might be toward,[21] that this sweaty haste   [21]*coming*

Doth make the night joint-labourer with the day?

Who is't that can inform me?

HORATIO: That can I;

At least the whisper goes so. Our last King,

95 Whose image even but now appear'd to us,

Was, as you know, by Fortinbras† of Norway,

Thereto prick'd[22] on by a most emulate[23] pride,   [22]*urged*

Dared to the combat; in which our valiant Hamlet—   [23]*ambitious*

For so this side of our known world esteem'd him—

†Terms marked in the text with (†) can be looked up in the Glossary for additional
information.

24*portion*

25*measured out*

26*would have*

27*untested*

28*outskirts*

29*hastily gathered*

30*grievances*

31*courage*

32*of force*

33*hurry*

34*commotion*

35*ominous*

36*tiny speck*

37*thriving*

38*the Roman dicta-
tor Julius Caesar*†

39*moon*

40*under*

41*the ancient Greek
god of the sea*

42*advance sign*

43*indicators*

44*region*

100   Did slay this Fortinbras; who by a seal'd compact,
       Well ratified by law and heraldry,
       Did forfeit, with his life, all those his lands
       Which he stood seized of, to the conqueror;
       Against the which, a moiety²⁴ competent
105   Was gaged²⁵ by our King; which had²⁶ return'd
       To the inheritance of Fortinbras,
       Had he been vanquisher, as, by the same covenant
       And carriage of the article design'd,
       His fell to Hamlet. Now, sir, young Fortinbras,
110   Of unimproved²⁷ metal hot and full,
       Hath in the skirts²⁸ of Norway here and there,
       Shark'd²⁹ up a list of lawless resolutes,³⁰
       For food and diet to some enterprise
       That hath a stomach³¹ in't; which is no other—
115   As it doth well appear unto our state—
       But to recover of us, by strong hand
       And terms compulsatory,³² those foresaid lands
       So by his father lost. And this, I take it,
       Is the main motive of our preparations,
120   The source of this our watch and the chief head
       Of this post-haste³³ and romage³⁴ in the land.
BERNARDO: I think it be no other but e'en so.
       Well may it sort that this portentous³⁵ figure
       Comes armed through our watch, so like the King
125   That was and is the question of these wars.
HORATIO: A mote³⁶ it is to trouble the mind's eye.   *Allusion*
       In the most high and palmy³⁷ state of Rome,
       A little ere the mightiest Julius³⁸ fell,
       The graves stood tenantless, and the sheeted dead
130   Did squeak and gibber in the Roman streets;
       As stars with trains of fire and dews of blood,
       Disasters in the sun; and the moist³⁹ star,
       Upon⁴⁰ whose influence Neptune's⁴¹ empire stands
       Was sick almost to doomsday with eclipse.
135   And even the like precurse⁴² of feared events,
       As harbingers⁴³ preceding still the fates
       And prologue to the omen coming on,
       Have heaven and earth together demonstrated
       Unto our climature⁴⁴ and countrymen.

Enter Ghost again.

140   But soft! behold! Lo, where it comes again!
         I'll cross it, though it blast me. Stay illusion!
         If thou hast any sound, or use of voice,
         Speak to me;
         If there be any good thing to be done,
145   That may to thee do ease and grace to me,[45]
         Speak to me;
         If thou art privy to thy country's fate,
         Which, happily, foreknowing may avoid,
         O, speak!
150   Or if thou hast uphoarded in thy life
         Extorted[46] treasure in the womb of earth,
         For which, they say, you spirits oft walk in death,
         Speak of it! stay, and speak! *[The cock crows.]* Stop it,
              Marcellus!
155 MARCELLUS: Shall I strike at it with my partisan?[47]
    HORATIO: Do, if it will not stand.
    BERNARDO: 'Tis here!
    HORATIO: 'Tis here!
    MARCELLUS: 'Tis gone!   *Exit Ghost.*
160   We do it wrong, being so majestical,
         To offer it the show of violence;
         For it is, as the air, invulnerable,
         And our vain blows malicious mockery.
    BERNARDO: It was about to speak, when the cock crew.
165 HORATIO: And then it started,[48] like a guilty thing
         Upon a fearful summons. I have heard
         The cock, that is the trumpet to the morn,
         Doth with his lofty and shrill-sounding throat
         Awake the god of day, and at his warning,
170   Whether in sea or fire, in earth or air,
         The extravagant[49] and erring spirit hies[50]
         To his confine;[51] and of the truth herein
         This present object made probation.[52]
    MARCELLUS: It faded on the crowing of the cock.
175   Some say that ever, 'gainst that season comes
         Wherein our Saviour's birth is celebrated,
         The bird of dawning[53] singeth all night long;
         And then, they say, no spirit dare stir abroad,

[45] *As a Catholic, Horatio believes his good works can help release the ghost from hell.*

[46] *wrongly gained*

[47] *spear*

[48] *jumped*

[49] *straying*

[50] *hurries*

[51] *prison*

[52] *proof*

[53] *rooster*

The nights are wholesome, then no planets strike,

180 No fairy takes, nor witch hath power to charm,

So hallow'd and so gracious is the time.

HORATIO: So have I heard and do in part believe it.

⁵⁴red

But look, the morn, in russet⁵⁴ mantle clad,

Walks o'er the dew of yon high eastward hill.

185 Break we our watch up; and by my advice

Let us impart what we have seen tonight

Unto young Hamlet; for, upon my life,

This spirit, dumb to us, will speak to him.

Do you consent we shall acquaint him with it,

190 As needful in our loves, fitting our duty?

MARCELLUS: Let's do't, I pray: and I this morning know

⁵⁵easily

Where we shall find him most conveniently.⁵⁵

Exeunt.

[SCENE II]

[A room of state in the Castle.]

Flourish. Enter Claudius, King of Denmark, Gertrude the Queen, [Hamlet, Polonius, his son Laertes [his sister Ophelia], Voltimand, Cornelius, Lords Attendant.]

KING: Though yet of Hamlet our dear brother's death

⁵⁶fresh

The memory be green,⁵⁶ and that it us befitted

To bear our hearts in grief and our whole kingdom

To be contracted in one brow of woe,

5 Yet so far hath discretion fought with nature

That we with wisest sorrow think on him

Together with remembrance of ourselves.

Therefore our sometime sister, now our queen, Motif

⁵⁷*the woman who holds right of inheritance*

The imperial jointress⁵⁷ to this warlike state,

10 Have we, as 'twere with a defeated joy,

With an auspicious, and a dropping eye,

⁵⁸*funeral song*

With mirth in funeral, and with dirge⁵⁸ in marriage,

⁵⁹*sorrow*

In equal scale weighing delight and dole,⁵⁹

Taken to wife. Nor have we herein barr'd

15 Your better wisdoms, which have freely gone

With this affair along. For all, our thanks.
Now follows, that you know, young Fortinbras,
Holding a weak supposal of our worth,
Or thinking by our late dear brother's death

20   Our state to be disjoint[60] and out of frame,
Colleagued[61] with this dream of his advantage,
He hath not fail'd to pester us with message,
Importing[62] the surrender of those lands
Lost by his father, with all bonds of law,

25   To our most valiant brother. So much for him.
Now for ourself, and for this time of meeting.
Thus much the business is: we have here writ
To Norway, uncle of young Fortinbras—
Who, impotent and bed-rid, scarcely hears

30   Of this his nephew's purpose—to suppress
His further gait[63] herein, in that the levies,[64]
The lists, and full proportions, are all made
Out of his subject; and we here dispatch
You, good Cornelius, and you, Voltimand,

35   For bearers of this greeting to old Norway,
Giving to you no further personal power
To business with the King, more than the scope
Of these dilated[65] articles allow.
Farewell, and let your haste commend your duty.

40   CORNELIUS, VOLTIMAND: In that and all things will we show
      our duty.
    KING: We doubt it nothing. Heartily farewell.

                [Exit Voltimand and Cornelius.]

And now, Laertes, what's the news with you?
You told us of some suit. What is't, Laertes?

45   You cannot speak of reason to the Dane,
And lose your voice. What wouldst thou beg, Laertes,
That shall not be my offer, not thy asking?
The head is not more native to the heart,
The hand more instrumental to the mouth,

50   Than is the throne of Denmark to thy father.
What wouldst thou have, Laertes?
    LAERTES: Dread my lord,
Your leave and favour to return to France;
From whence though willingly I came to Denmark,

---

[60] *disorganized*

[61] *joined*

[62] *regarding*

[63] *steps (i.e., course of action)*

[64] *gathered forces*

[65] *explanatory*

55   To show my duty in your coronation,
Yet now, I must confess, that duty done,
My thoughts and wishes bend again toward France
And bow them to your gracious leave and pardon.
KING: Have you your father's leave? What says Polonius?
60 POLONIUS: He hath, my lord, wrung from me my slow leave

Is supposed to be Funny. Repeats everything

By laboursome petition, and at last
Upon his will I seal'd my hard consent.
I do beseech you, give him leave to go.
KING: Take thy fair hour, Laertes. Time be thine,
65   And thy best graces spend it at thy will!
But now, my cousin Hamlet, and my son,—

Pun & Incest

HAMLET: A little more than kin, and less than kind!

Family

KING: How is it that the clouds still hang on you?
HAMLET: Not so, my lord: I am too much i' the sun.
70 QUEEN: Good Hamlet, cast thy nighted color off,
And let thine eye look like a friend on Denmark.
Do not for ever with thy vailed lids
Seek for thy noble father in the dust.
Thou know'st 'tis common. All that lives must die,
75   Passing through nature to eternity.
HAMLET: Ay, madam, it is common.
QUEEN: If it be,
Why seems it so particular with thee?
HAMLET: Seems, madam? Nay, it is. I know not seems.
80   'Tis not alone my inky cloak, good mother,
Nor customary suits of solemn black,
Nor windy suspiration[66] of forced breath,
No, nor the fruitful river in the eye,
Nor the dejected havior[67] of the visage,
85   Together with all forms, modes, shapes of grief,
That can denote me truly. These indeed seem,
For they are actions that a man might play;
But I have that within which passeth show,
These but the trappings and the suits of woe.
90 KING: 'Tis sweet and commendable in your nature, Hamlet,
To give these mourning duties to your father;
But you must know, your father lost a father;
That father lost, lost his, and the survivor bound
In filial obligation for some term

saying everyones dad dies

[66]*sighing*

[67]*manner*

95   To do obsequious sorrow. But to persever

saying God wants him to stop

In obstinate condolement[68] is a course

     [68]*misery*

Of impious stubbornness; 'tis unmanly grief;

It shows a will most incorrect to heaven,

A heart unfortified, a mind impatient,

100   An understanding simple and unschool'd;

For what we know must be, and is as common

As any the most vulgar thing to sense,

Why should we, in our peevish opposition, *Anaphora*

Take it to heart? Fie! 'tis a fault to heaven,

105   A fault against the dead, a fault to nature,

To reason most absurd, whose common theme

Is death of fathers, and who still hath cried,

From the first corse[69] till he that died today,   [69]*corpse*

This must be so. We pray you throw to earth *Purpose of*

110   This unprevailing woe, and think of us   *passage*

As of a father; for let the world take note

You are the most immediate to our throne, *Insult*

And with no less nobility of love

Than that which dearest father bears his son

115   Do I impart toward you. For your intent

In going back to school in Wittenberg,[70]   [70]*a city in Germany*[†]

It is most retrograde[71] to our desire;   [71]*contrary*

And we beseech you, bend you to remain

Here in the cheer and comfort of our eye,

120   Our chiefest courtier, cousin, and our son.

QUEEN: Let not thy mother lose her prayers, Hamlet.

I pray thee, stay with us, go not to Wittenberg.

HAMLET: I shall in all my best obey you, madam.

KING: Why, 'tis a loving and a fair reply.

125   Be as ourself in Denmark. Madam, come.

This gentle and unforced accord of Hamlet

Sits smiling to my heart; in grace whereof,

No jocund health that Denmark drinks today

But the great cannon to the clouds shall tell,

130   And the King's rouse[72] the heaven shall bruit[73] again,   [72]*noisy drinking*

Re-speaking earthly thunder. Come away.   [73]*announce, echo*

Flourish. Exeunt all but Hamlet.

HAMLET: O, that this too too sullied flesh would melt,

Thaw and resolve itself into a dew,

74*law*

135   Or that the Everlasting had not fix'd
His canon74 'gainst self-slaughter! O God! God!
How weary, stale, flat and unprofitable
Seem to me all the uses of this world!
Fie on't! ah, fie! 'Tis an unweeded garden
That grows to seed; things rank and gross in nature
140   Possess it merely. That it should come to this!
But two months dead! Nay, not so much, not two;
So excellent a king, that was, to this,

75*the sun god*†

Hyperion75 to a satyr;76 so loving to my mother

76*half-human, half-goat*†

That he might not beteem77 the winds of heaven

77*allow*

145   Visit her face too roughly. Heaven and earth!
Must I remember? Why, she would hang on him
As if increase of appetite had grown
By what it fed on; and yet, within a month—
Let me not think on't! Frailty, thy name is woman—
150   A little month, or ere those shoes were old
With which she follow'd my poor father's body
Like Niobe,† all tears—why she, even she—

78*lacks*

O God! a beast that wants78 discourse of reason
Would have mourn'd longer—married with my uncle,
155   My father's brother, but no more like my father

79*the strongest man in the world*†

Than I to Hercules.79 Within a month,
Ere yet the salt of most unrighteous tears

80*swollen*

Had left the flushing in her galled80 eyes,
She married. O, most wicked speed, to post

81*quickness*

160   With such dexterity81 to incestuous sheets!
It is not, nor it cannot come to, good.
But break, my heart, for I must hold my tongue!

Enter Horatio, Marcellus, and Bernardo.

HORATIO: Hail to your lordship!
HAMLET: I am glad to see you well.
165   Horatio—or I do forget myself.
HORATIO: The same, my lord, and your poor servant ever.
HAMLET: Sir, my good friend; I'll change that name with you.
    And what make you from Wittenberg, Horatio?—
    Marcellus?
170 MARCELLUS: My good lord!

HAMLET: I am very glad to see you.— *[To Bernardo]* Good
    even, sir.—

    But what, in faith, make you from Wittenberg?

HORATIO: A truant[82] disposition, good my lord.   *[82]negligent*

175 HAMLET: I would not hear your enemy say so,
    Nor shall you do my ear that violence
    To make it truster of your own report
    Against yourself. I know you are no truant.
    But what is your affair in Elsinore?

180   We'll teach you to drink deep ere you depart.

HORATIO: My lord, I came to see your father's funeral.

HAMLET: I prithee do not mock me, fellow student.
    I think it was to see my mother's wedding.

HORATIO: Indeed, my lord, it followed hard upon.

185 HAMLET: Thrift, thrift, Horatio. The funeral baked meats
    Did coldly furnish forth the marriage tables.
    Would I had met my dearest foe in heaven
    Or ever I had seen that day, Horatio!
    My father—methinks I see my father.

190 HORATIO: O, where, my lord?

HAMLET: In my mind's eye, Horatio.

HORATIO: I saw him once. He was a goodly king.

HAMLET: He was a man, take him for all in all;
    I shall not look upon his like again.

195 HORATIO: My lord, I think I saw him yesternight.

HAMLET: Saw? Who?

HORATIO: My lord, the King your father.   *saw his fathers ghost saying he*

HAMLET: The King my father?

HORATIO: Season[83] your admiration for a while   *[83]control*

200   With an attent ear, till I may deliver
    Upon the witness of these gentlemen,
    This marvel to you.

HAMLET: For God's love let me hear!

HORATIO: Two nights together had these gentlemen

205   Marcellus and Bernardo, on their watch
    In the dead vast and middle of the night,
    Been thus encountered. A figure like your father,
    Armed at point exactly, cap-à-pie,[84]   *[84]from head to toe*
    Appears before them, and with solemn march

210   Goes slow and stately by them. Thrice he walk'd

[85]heavy club's

By their oppress'd and fear-surprised eyes,
Within his truncheon's[85] length; whilst they, distill'd
Almost to jelly with the act of fear,
Stand dumb and speak not to him. This to me
215   In dreadful secrecy impart they did,
And I with them the third night kept the watch;
Where, as they had deliver'd, both in time,
Form of the thing, each word made true and good,
The apparition comes. I knew your father.
220   These hands are not more like.
       HAMLET: But where was this?
       MARCELLUS: My lord, upon the platform where we watch'd.
       HAMLET: Did you not speak to it?
       HORATIO: My lord, I did;
225   But answer made it none. Yet once methought
It lifted up its head and did address
Itself to motion, like as it would speak;
But, even then, the morning cock crew loud,
And at the sound it shrunk in haste away
230   And vanish'd from our sight.
       HAMLET: 'Tis very strange.
       HORATIO: As I do live, my honour'd lord, 'tis true;
And we did think it writ down in our duty
To let you know of it.
235   HAMLET: Indeed, indeed, sirs. But this troubles me.
Hold you the watch tonight?
       MARCELLUS AND BERNARDO: We do, my lord.
       HAMLET: Arm'd, say you?
       MARCELLUS AND BERNARDO: Arm'd, my lord.
240   HAMLET: From top to toe?
       MARCELLUS AND BERNARDO: My lord, from head to foot.
       HAMLET: Then saw you not his face?
       HORATIO: O, yes, my lord! He wore his beaver[86] up.   Face sheild
       HAMLET: What, look'd he frowningly?
245   HORATIO: A countenance more in sorrow than in anger.
       HAMLET: Pale, or red?
       HORATIO: Nay, very pale.
       HAMLET: And fix'd his eyes upon you?
       HORATIO: Most constantly.
250   HAMLET: I would I had been there.
       HORATIO: It would have much amazed you.

[86]visor

HAMLET: Very like, very like. Stay'd it long?

HORATIO: While one with moderate haste might tell a hundred.

MARCELLUS AND BERNARDO: Longer, longer.

255 HORATIO: Not when I saw't.

HAMLET: His beard was grizzled, no?

HORATIO: It was as I have seen it in his life,
    A sable[87] silvered.

HAMLET: I will watch tonight.

260   Perchance 'twill walk again.

HORATIO: I warrant it will.

HAMLET: If it assume my noble father's person,
    I'll speak to it, though hell itself should gape
    And bid me hold my peace. I pray you all,
265   If you have hitherto conceal'd this sight,
    Let it be tenable[88] in your silence still;
    And whatsoever else shall hap tonight,
    Give it an understanding, but no tongue.
    I will requite your loves. So, fare you well.
270   Upon the platform, 'twixt eleven and twelve,
    I'll visit you.

ALL: Our duty to your honour.

Exeunt [all but Hamlet.]

HAMLET: Your loves, as mine to you. Farewell.
    My father's spirit in arms! All is not well.
275   I doubt some foul play. Would the night were come.
    Till then sit still, my soul. Foul deeds will rise,
    Though all the earth o'erwhelm them, to men's eyes.

Exit.

87black

88held

[SCENE III]
[A room in the house of Polonius.]

Enter Laertes, and Ophelia, his sister.

LAERTES: My necessaries are embark'd.[89] Farewell.
    And, sister, as the winds give benefit
    And convoy[90] is assistant,[91] do not sleep,
    But let me hear from you.

5 OPHELIA: Do you doubt that?

89on the ship

90transportation

91convenient

[92] *passing phase*

[93] *diversion*

[94] *muscles*

[95] *along with it*

[96] *deceit*

[97] *make dirty*

[98] *confined*

[99] *believing*

[100] *persistence (in asking)*

[101] *most cautious*

[102] *reckless*

[103] *worm*

[104] *revealed*

[105] *plagues*

LAERTES: For Hamlet, and the trifling of his favours,
     Hold it a fashion,[92] and a toy in blood;
     A violet in the youth of primy nature,
     Forward, not permanent, sweet, not lasting;
10   The perfume and suppliance[93] of a minute;
     No more.
OPHELIA: No more but so?
LAERTES: Think it no more.
     For nature, crescent, does not grow alone
15   In thews[94] and bulk; but as this temple waxes,
     The inward service of the mind and soul
     Grows wide withal.[95] Perhaps he loves you now,
     And now no soil nor cautel[96] doth besmirch[97]
     The virtue of his will; but you must fear,
20   His greatness weigh'd, his will is not his own;
     For he himself is subject to his birth.
     He may not, as unvalued persons do,
     Carve for himself; for on his choice depends
     The safety and health of this whole state,
25   And therefore must his choice be circumscribed[98]
     Unto the voice and yielding of that body
     Whereof he is the head. Then if he says he loves you,
     It fits your wisdom so far to believe it
     As he in his particular act and place
30   May give his saying deed; which is no further
     Than the main voice of Denmark goes withal.
     Then weigh what loss your honour may sustain
     If with too credent[99] ear you list his songs,
     Or lose your heart, or your chaste treasure open
35   To his unmaster'd importunity.[100]
     Fear it, Ophelia, fear it, my dear sister,
     And keep you in the rear of your affection,
     Out of the shot and danger of desire.
     The chariest[101] maid is prodigal[102] enough
40   If she unmask her beauty to the moon.
     Virtue itself 'scapes not calumnious strokes.
     The canker[103] galls the infants of the spring
     Too oft before their buttons be disclosed,[104]
     And in the morn and liquid dew of youth
45   Contagious blastments[105] are most imminent.

[Handwritten margin notes:]

God knows if you open up yourself to him.

If you sleep with Hamlet when you're young you'll probably get a STD.

Be wary then; best safety lies in fear.
Youth to itself rebels, though none else near.
OPHELIA: I shall the effect of this good lesson keep
As watchman to my heart. But, good my brother,
50   Do not, as some ungracious pastors do,
Show me the steep and thorny way to heaven,
Whilst, like a puff'd and reckless libertine,[106]
Himself the primrose path of dalliance[107] treads
And recks[108] not his own rede.[109]
55 LAERTES: O, fear me not!

Enter Polonius.

I stay too long. But here my father comes.
A double blessing is a double grace;
Occasion smiles upon a second leave.
POLONIUS: Yet here, Laertes? Aboard, aboard, for shame!
60   The wind sits in the shoulder of your sail,
And you are stay'd for. There, my blessing with thee.
And these few precepts in thy memory
See thou character. Give thy thoughts no tongue,
Nor any unproportion'd[110] thought his act.
65   Be thou familiar, but by no means vulgar.
Those friends thou hast, and their adoption tried,[111]
Grapple[112] them to thy soul with hoops of steel;
But do not dull thy palm with entertainment
Of each new-hatch'd, unfledged comrade. Beware
70   Of entrance to a quarrel; but being in,
Bear't[113] that the opposed may beware of thee.
Give every man thy ear, but few thy voice;
Take each man's censure, but reserve thy judgment.
Costly thy habit as thy purse can buy,
75   But not express'd in fancy; rich, not gaudy;
For the apparel oft proclaims the man,
And they in France of the best rank and station
Are of a most select and generous chief in that.[114]
Neither a borrower nor a lender be;
80   For loan oft loses both itself and friend,
And borrowing dulls the edge of husbandry.[115]
This above all: to thine own self be true,
And it must follow, as the night the day,

[106]*one who acts without restraint*
[107]*indulgence*
[108]*follows*
[109]*advice*
[110]*inappropriate*
[111]*tested*
[112]*fasten*
[113]*keep in mind*
[114]*their apparel*
[115]*money management*

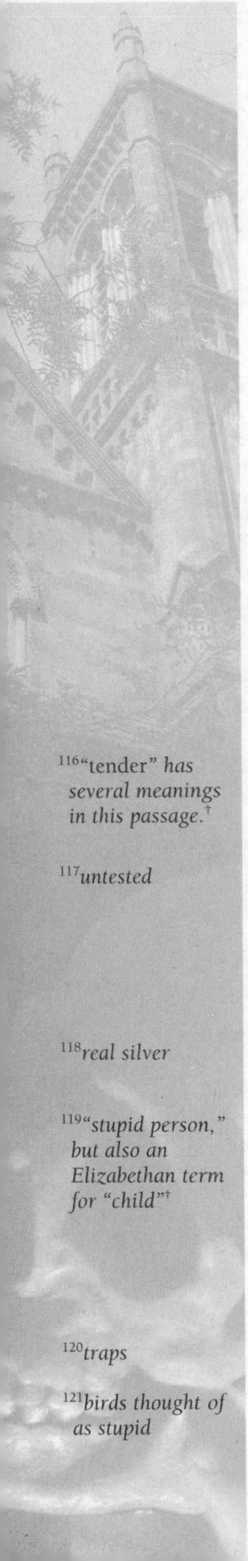

Thou canst not then be false to any man.

85 Farewell. My blessing season this in thee!

LAERTES: Most humbly do I take my leave, my lord.

POLONIUS: The time invites you. Go, your servants tend.

LAERTES: Farewell, Ophelia, and remember well

What I have said to you.

90 OPHELIA: 'Tis in my memory lock'd,

And you yourself shall keep the key of it.

LAERTES: Farewell.   *Exit Laertes.*

POLONIUS: What is't, Ophelia, he hath said to you?

OPHELIA: So please you, something touching the Lord

95   Hamlet.

POLONIUS: Marry, well bethought!

'Tis told me, he hath very oft of late

Given private time to you, and you yourself

Have of your audience been most free and bounteous.

100 If it be so— as so 'tis put on me,

And that in way of caution—I must tell you,

You do not understand yourself so clearly

As it behooves my daughter and your honour.

What is between you? Give me up the truth.

105 OPHELIA: He hath, my lord, of late made many tenders[116]

Of his affection to me.

POLONIUS: Affection? Pooh! You speak like a green girl,

Unsifted[117] in such perilous circumstance.

Do you believe his tenders, as you call them?

110 OPHELIA: I do not know, my lord, what I should think.

POLONIUS: Marry, I'll teach you. Think yourself a baby,

That you have ta'en these tenders for true pay,

Which are not sterling.[118] Tender yourself more dearly,

Or—not to crack the wind of the poor phrase,

115 Running it thus—you'll tender me a fool.[119]

OPHELIA: My lord, he hath importuned me with love

In honourable fashion.

POLONIUS: Ay, fashion you may call it. Go to, go to!

OPHELIA: And hath given countenance to his speech, my

120   lord,

With almost all the holy vows of heaven.

POLONIUS: Ay, springes[120] to catch woodcocks.[121] I do know,

When the blood burns, how prodigal the soul

---

[116]"tender" has several meanings in this passage.†

[117]untested

[118]real silver

[119]"stupid person," but also an Elizabethan term for "child"†

[120]traps

[121]birds thought of as stupid

[Handwritten margin note:] Play hard to get

[Handwritten note at bottom:] When you're horny you talk a big game

Lends the tongue vows. These blazes, daughter,
125   Giving more light than heat, extinct in both
Even in their promise, as it is a-making,
You must not take for fire. From this time
Be something scanter[122] of your maiden presence.   [122]*less generous*
Set your entreatments[123] at a higher rate   [123]*negotiations*
130   Than a command to parley.[124] For Lord Hamlet,   [124]*conference*†
Believe so much in him, that he is young,
And with a larger tether[125] may he walk   [125]*leash*
Than may be given you. In few, Ophelia,
Do not believe his vows; for they are brokers,[126]   [126]*agents*
135   Not of that dye which their investments[127] show,   [127]*clothes (i.e.,*
But mere implorators[128] of unholy suits,   *their outward*
Breathing like sanctified and pious bonds,   *appearance)*
The better to beguile. This is for all:
I would not, in plain terms, from this time forth   [128]*ones who beg*
140   Have you so slander any moment leisure[129]   [129]*idle*
As to give words or talk with the Lord Hamlet.
Look to't, I charge you. Come your ways.
OPHELIA: I shall obey, my lord.

Exeunt.

[handwritten annotation: People are going to cut him alot more slack since he's royalty.]

[SCENE IV]
[Elsinore. The platform before the Castle.]

Enter Hamlet, Horatio, and Marcellus.

HAMLET: The air bites shrewdly; it is very cold.
HORATIO: It is a nipping and an eager air.
HAMLET: What hour now?
HORATIO: I think it lacks of twelve.
5 MARCELLUS: No, it is struck.
HORATIO: Indeed? I heard it not. It then draws near the season
Wherein the spirit held his wont[130] to walk.   [130]*habit*
          A flourish of trumpets, and ordnance[131] go off.   [131]*cannons*
What doth this mean, my lord?
HAMLET: The King doth wake tonight and takes his rouse,

132*a drinking party*

133*German dance*

134*dances*

135*cups*

136*wine from the Rhineland*

137*breaking*

138*slandered*

139*call*

140*reputation*

141*core*

142*honor*

143*natural quality*

144*pleasing*

145*uniform*

146*judgment*

147*small amount*

10   Keeps wassail,[132] and the swaggering upspring[133] reels,[134]
     And as he drains his draughts[135] of Rhenish[136] down,
     The kettle-drum and trumpet thus bray out
     The triumph of his pledge.
     HORATIO: Is it a custom?
15   HAMLET: Ay, marry, is't;
     But to my mind, though I am native here
     And to the manner born, it is a custom
     More honour'd in the breach[137] than the observance.
     This heavy-headed revel, east and west,
20   Makes us traduced[138] and tax'd of other nations;
     They clepe[139] us drunkards and with swinish phrase
     Soil our addition;[140] and indeed it takes
     From our achievements, though perform'd at height,
     The pith[141] and marrow of our attribute.[142]
25   So, oft it chances in particular men,
     That for some vicious mole of nature in them,
     As in their birth—wherein they are not guilty,
     Since nature cannot choose his origin—
     By the o'ergrowth of some complexion,[143]
30   Oft breaking down the pales and forts of reason,
     Or by some habit that too much o'erleavens
     The form of plausive[144] manners, that these men—
     Carrying, I say, the stamp of one defect,
     Being nature's livery,[145] or fortune's star—
35   Their virtues else—be they as pure as grace,
     As infinite as man may undergo—
     Shall in the general censure[146] take corruption
     From that particular fault. The dram[147] of evil†
     Doth all the noble substance of a doubt
40   To his own scandal.

     Enter Ghost.

     HORATIO: Look, my lord, it comes!
     HAMLET: Angels and ministers of grace defend us!
         Be thou a spirit of health or goblin damn'd,
         Bring with thee airs from heaven or blasts from hell,
45   Be thy intents wicked or charitable,
         Thou comest in such a questionable shape
         That I will speak to thee. I'll call thee Hamlet,

King, father, royal Dane. O, answer me!
Let me not burst in ignorance, but tell
50   Why thy canonized[148] bones, hearsed[149] in death,
Have burst their cerements,[150] why the sepulchre[151]
Wherein we saw thee quietly inurn'd,[152]
Hath oped his ponderous and marble jaws
To cast thee up again. What may this mean
55   That thou, dead corse, again, in complete steel,
Revisits thus the glimpses of the moon,
Making night hideous, and we fools of nature
So horridly to shake our disposition
With thoughts beyond the reaches of our souls?
60   Say, why is this? Wherefore? What should we do?
                    [Ghost beckons Hamlet.]

HORATIO: It beckons you to go away with it,
As if it some impartment[153] did desire
To you alone.
MARCELLUS: Look with what courteous action
65   It waves you to a more removed ground.
But do not go with it!
HORATIO: No, by no means.
HAMLET: It will not speak; then will I follow it.
HORATIO: Do not, my lord!
70   HAMLET: Why, what should be the fear?
I do not set my life at a pin's fee;
And for my soul, what can it do to that,
Being a thing immortal as itself?
It waves me forth again. I'll follow it.
75   HORATIO: What if it tempt you toward the flood, my lord,
Or to the dreadful summit of the cliff
That beetles[154] o'er his base into the sea,
And there assume some other horrible form,
Which might deprive your sovereignty of reason
80   And draw you into madness? Think of it.
The very place puts toys of desperation,[155]
Without more motive, into every brain
That looks so many fathoms[156] to the sea
And hears it roar beneath.
85   HAMLET: It waves me still.
Go on; I'll follow thee.
MARCELLUS: You shall not go, my lord.

[148]*having under-
gone Christian
burial*†

[149]*laid in a coffin*

[150]*burial clothes*

[151]*grave*

[152]*buried*

[153]*communication*

[154]*protrudes*

[155]*crazy ideas*

[156]*A fathom is
equal to six feet.*

HAMLET: Hold off your hands!

HORATIO: Be ruled. You shall not go.

90 HAMLET: My fate cries out,

And makes each petty artery in this body

As hardy as the Nemean lion's[157] nerve.

[Ghost beckons.]

Still am I call'd. Unhand me, gentlemen.

By heaven, I'll make a ghost of him that lets me. *I'll turn you into a ghost if you try to stop me*

95   I say, away! Go on. I'll follow thee.

Exit Ghost and Hamlet.

HORATIO: He waxes[158] desperate with imagination.

MARCELLUS: Let's follow. 'Tis not fit thus to obey him.

HORATIO: Have after. To what issue will this come?

MARCELLUS: Something is rotten in the state of Denmark.

100 HORATIO: Heaven will direct it.

MARCELLUS: Nay, let's follow him.

Exeunt.

[157] *a mythological lion with enormous strength*[†]

[158] *grows*

[SCENE V]
[The Castle. Another part of the fortifications.]

Enter Ghost, and Hamlet.

HAMLET: Whither wilt thou lead me? Speak! I'll go no further.

GHOST: Mark me.

HAMLET: I will.

GHOST: My hour is almost come,

5   When I to sulphurous and tormenting flames *Hamlet thought his dad was good but he's in hell.*

Must render up myself.

HAMLET: Alas, poor ghost!

GHOST: Pity me not, but lend thy serious hearing

To what I shall unfold.

10 HAMLET: Speak; I am bound to hear.

GHOST: So art thou to revenge, when thou shalt hear.

HAMLET: What!

GHOST: I am thy father's spirit,

Doom'd for a certain term to walk the night,

15   And for the day confined to fast in fires,
Till the foul crimes done in my days of nature
Are burnt and purged away. But that I am forbid
To tell the secrets of my prison-house,
I could a tale unfold whose lightest word

20   Would harrow[159] up thy soul, freeze thy young blood,

> [159]torment

Make thy two eyes, like stars, start from their spheres,
Thy knotted and combined locks to part,
And each particular hair to stand an end
Like quills upon the fretful porpentine.[160]

> [160]porcupine

25   But this eternal blazon[161] must not be

> [161]revelation

To ears of flesh and blood. List, list, O, list!
If thou didst ever thy dear father love—

HAMLET: O God!

GHOST: Revenge his foul and most unnatural murder.

30 HAMLET: Murder?

GHOST: Murder most foul, as in the best it is;
But this most foul, strange, and unnatural.

HAMLET: Haste me to know't, that I, with wings as swift
As meditation or the thoughts of love,

35   May sweep to my revenge.

GHOST: I find thee apt;[162]

> *Hamlets dad said his uncle killed him.*

> [162]ready

And duller shouldst thou be than the fat weed
That roots itself in ease on Lethe[163] wharf,
Wouldst thou not stir in this. Now, Hamlet, hear.

> [163]*the river of forgetfulness in Greek mythology[T]*

40   'Tis given out that, sleeping in mine orchard,
A serpent stung me. So the whole ear of Denmark
Is by a forged process of my death
Rankly abused. But know, thou noble youth,
The serpent that did sting thy father's life

45   Now wears his crown.

HAMLET: O my prophetic soul! My uncle!

GHOST: Ay, that incestuous, that adulterate beast,
With witchcraft of his wit, with traitorous gifts—
O wicked wit and gifts, that have the power

50   So to seduce!—won to his shameful lust
The will of my most seeming-virtuous queen.

> *Saying he wish Claudiece wasn't so sexy.*

O Hamlet, what a falling off was there!
From me, whose love was of that dignity
That it went hand in hand even with the vow

55   I made to her in marriage, and to decline
      Upon a wretch, whose natural gifts were poor
      To those of mine.
      But virtue, as it never will be moved,
      Though lewdness court it in a shape of heaven,
60   So lust, though to a radiant angel link'd,
      Will sate itself in a celestial bed
      And prey on garbage.

Saying the queen is sleeping with a bed of garbage

      But soft! methinks I scent the morning air.
      Brief let me be. Sleeping within my orchard,
65   My custom always of the afternoon,
      Upon my secure hour thy uncle stole,
      With juice of cursed hebenon[164] in a vial,
      And in the porches of my ears did pour
      The leperous[165] distilment,[166] whose effect
70   Holds such an enmity with blood of man
      That, swift as quicksilver,[167] it courses through
      The natural gates and alleys of the body,
      And, with a sudden vigour, it doth posset[168]
      And curd, like eager droppings into milk,
75   The thin and wholesome blood. So did it mine;
      And a most instant tetter[169] bark'd[170] about,
      Most lazar[171]-like, with vile and loathsome crust
      All my smooth body.
      Thus was I, sleeping, by a brother's hand
80   Of life, of crown, of queen, at once dispatch'd;
      Cut off even in the blossoms of my sin,
      Unhouseled,[172] disappointed, unaneled,[173]
      No reckoning[174] made, but sent to my account
      With all my imperfections on my head.
85   HAMLET: O, horrible! O, horrible! most horrible!
      GHOST: If thou hast nature in thee, bear it not.
      Let not the royal bed of Denmark be
      A couch for luxury and damned incest.
      But, howsoever thou pursuest this act,

Act is to murder uncle

90   Taint not thy mind, nor let thy soul contrive
      Against thy mother aught.[175] Leave her to heaven,
      And to those thorns that in her bosom lodge
      To prick and sting her. Fare thee well at once.

Leave mother alone

      The glow-worm shows the matin[176] to be near
95   And 'gins to pale his uneffectual fire.

[164]*poisonous plant*

[165]*causing sores*

[166]*potion*

[167]*mercury†*

[168]*clot*

[169]*skin eruption*

[170]*crusted*

[171]*leper*

[172]*without Holy Communion†*

[173]*without Last Rites†*

[174]*account of my sin*

[175]*at all*

[176]*morning*

to god

Adieu, adieu, adieu! Remember me.   *[Exit.]*

HAMLET: O all you host of heaven! O earth! What else?
And shall I couple[177] hell? O, fie! Hold, hold, my heart!   [177]*add*
And you, my sinews,[178] grow not instant old,   [178]*muscles*

100   But bear me stiffly up. Remember thee?
Ay, thou poor ghost, while memory holds a seat   *saying to murder*
In this distracted globe.[179] Remember thee?   [179]*mind*
Yea, from the table of my memory   *king & send him*
I'll wipe away all trivial fond[180] records,   *to god* [180]*foolish*

105   All saws of books, all forms, all pressures[181] past, [181]*impressions*
That youth and observation copied there;
And thy commandment all alone shall live
Within the book and volume of my brain,
Unmix'd with baser matter. Yes, by heaven!

110   O most pernicious[182] woman!   [182]*evil*
O villain, villain, smiling, damned villain!   *Lots of repeating*
My tables—meet[183] it is I set it down   [183]*suitable*
That one may smile, and smile, and be a villain;
At least I am sure it may be so in Denmark.

115   So, uncle, there you are. Now to my word: *Just very*
It is 'Adieu, adieu! Remember me.'   *mad at his*
I have sworn't.   *uncle*

Enter Horatio and Marcellus.

HORATIO: My lord, my lord!
MARCELLUS: Lord Hamlet!

120 HORATIO: Heaven secure him!
HAMLET: So be it!
MARCELLUS: Illo, ho, ho, my lord!
HAMLET: Hillo, ho, ho, boy! Come, bird, come.
MARCELLUS: How is't, my noble lord?

125 HORATIO: What news, my lord?
MARCELLUS: O, wonderful!
HORATIO: Good my lord, tell it.
HAMLET: No; you will reveal it.
HORATIO: Not I, my lord, by heaven!

130 MARCELLUS: Nor I, my lord.
HAMLET: How say you, then; would heart of man once think it?
But you'll be secret?
HORATIO AND MARCELLUS: Ay, by heaven, my lord.

HAMLET: There's ne'er a villain dwelling in all Denmark

135   But he's an arrant knave.[184]

HORATIO: There needs no ghost, my lord, come from the grave

To tell us this.

HAMLET: Why, right! You are in the right!

140   And so, without more circumstance at all,

I hold it fit that we shake hands and part;

You, as your business and desire shall point you—

For every man hath business and desire,

Such as it is; and for my own poor part,

145   Look you, I'll go pray.

HORATIO: These are but wild and whirling words, my lord.

HAMLET: I am sorry they offend you, heartily;

Yes, faith, heartily.

HORATIO: There's no offence, my lord.

150   HAMLET: Yes, by Saint Patrick, but there is, Horatio,

And much offence too. Touching this vision here,

It is an honest ghost, that let me tell you.

For your desire to know what is between us,

O'ermaster't as you may. And now, good friends,

155   As you are friends, scholars, and soldiers,

Give me one poor request.

HORATIO: What is't, my lord? We will.

HAMLET: Never make known what you have seen to-night.

MARCELLUS AND HORATIO: My lord, we will not.

160   HAMLET: Nay, but swear't.

HORATIO: In faith,

My lord, not I.

MARCELLUS: Nor I, my lord, in faith.

HAMLET: Upon my sword.

165   MARCELLUS: We have sworn, my lord, already.

HAMLET: Indeed, upon my sword, indeed.

GHOST: *[Ghost cries under the stage.]* Swear.

HAMLET: Ah, ha boy, say'st thou so? Art thou there,
            truepenny?[185]

170   Come on! You hear this fellow in the cellarage.

Consent to swear.

HORATIO: Propose the oath, my lord.

HAMLET: Never to speak of this that you have seen.

Swear by my sword.

184*scoundrel*

185*honest fellow*

175 GHOST: Swear.

HAMLET: *Hic et ubique?*[186] Then we'll shift our ground.
Come hither, gentlemen,
And lay your hands again upon my sword.
Never to speak of this that you have heard:
180 Swear by my sword.

GHOST: Swear.

HAMLET: Well said, old mole! Canst work i' the earth so fast?
A worthy pioner![187] Once more remove, good friends.

HORATIO: O day and night, but this is wondrous strange!

185 HAMLET: And therefore as a stranger give it welcome.
There are more things in heaven and earth, Horatio,
Than are dreamt of in your philosophy.
But come!
Here, as before, never, so help you mercy,
190 How strange or odd soe'er I bear myself—
As I perchance hereafter shall think meet
To put an antic[188] disposition on—
That you, at such times seeing me, never shall,
With arms encumber'd thus, or this head shake,
195 Or by pronouncing of some doubtful phrase,
As "Well, well, we know," or "We could, an if we would,"
Or "If we list to speak" or "There be, an if they might,"
Or such ambiguous giving out, to note
That you know aught of me; this is not to do,
200 So grace and mercy at your most need help you,
Swear.

GHOST: Swear.

HAMLET: Rest, rest, perturbed spirit! So, gentlemen,
With all my love I do commend me to you;
205 And what so poor a man as Hamlet is
May do to express his love and friendling to you,
God willing, shall not lack. Let us go in together;
And still your fingers on your lips, I pray.
The time is out of joint. O cursed spite,
210 That ever I was born to set it right!
Nay, come, let's go together.

Exeunt.

[186] *here and every-where*

[187] *digger*

[188] *abnormal, crazy*

[handwritten] Hamlet is going to act crazy now.

[handwritten] Hamlet is warning his friends

ACT II

[SCENE I]
[Elsinore. A room in the house of Polonius.]

Enter old Polonius with his man [Reynaldo] or two.

POLONIUS: Give him this money and these notes, Reynaldo.
REYNALDO: I will, my lord.
POLONIUS: You shall do marvellous wisely, good Reynaldo,
    Before you visit him, to make inquire
5   Of his behaviour.
REYNALDO: My lord, I did intend it.
POLONIUS: Marry, well said, very well said. Look you, sir,
    Inquire me first what Danskers[1] are in Paris,
    And how, and who, what means, and where they keep,
10   What company, at what expense; and finding
    By this encompassment[2] and drift of question
    That they do know my son, come you more nearer
    Than your particular demands will touch it.
    Take you, as 'twere, some distant knowledge of him,
15   As thus, 'I know his father and his friends,
    And in part him.' Do you mark this, Reynaldo?
REYNALDO: Ay, very well, my lord.
POLONIUS: 'And in part him, but,' you may say, 'not well.
    But if't be he I mean, he's very wild,
20   Addicted so and so'; and there put on him
    What forgeries you please—marry, none so rank
    As may dishonour him, take heed of that—
    But, sir, such wanton,[3] wild and usual slips
    As are companions noted and most known
25   To youth and liberty.
REYNALDO: As gaming, my lord?

[1]*Danes*

[2]*roundabout talking*

[3]*undisciplined*

[handwritten note: Polonius telling Reynaldo to talk shit about his son]

41

POLONIUS: Ay, or drinking, fencing, swearing, quarrelling,
  Drabbing.[4] You may go so far.
REYNALDO: My lord, that would dishonour him.

30 POLONIUS: Faith, no; as you may season[5] it in the charge.
  You must not put another scandal on him,
  That he is open to incontinency.[6]
  That's not my meaning; but breathe his faults so quaintly[7]
  That they may seem the taints of liberty,
35 The flash and outbreak of a fiery mind,
  A savageness in unreclaimed blood,
  Of general assault.
REYNALDO: But, my good lord—
POLONIUS: Wherefore should you do this?

40 REYNALDO: Ay, my lord,
  I would know that.
POLONIUS: Marry, sir, here's my drift,
  And I believe it is a fetch[8] of warrant.[9]
  You laying these slight sullies on my son
45 As 'twere a thing a little soil'd i' the working,
  Mark you,
  Your party in converse, him you would sound,
  Having ever seen in the prenominate[10] crimes
  The youth you breathe of guilty, be assured
50 He closes with you in this consequence:
  'Good sir,' or so, or 'friend,' or 'gentleman'
  According to the phrase or the addition
  Of man and country
REYNALDO: Very good, my lord.

55 POLONIUS: And then, sir, does he this—he does—what was I
    about to say?
  By the mass, I was about to say something! Where did I
    leave?
REYNALDO: At 'closes in the consequence,' at 'friend or so,' and
60 gentleman.'
POLONIUS: At 'closes in the consequence,' ay, marry!
  He closes with you thus: 'I know the gentleman.
  I saw him yesterday,' or 't'other day,'
  Or then, or then, with such, or such; 'and, as you say,
65 There was a gaming,' 'there o'ertook in's rouse,'
  'There falling out at tennis'; or perchance,

If they agree they know Polonius is up to no good

'I saw him enter such a house of sale,'
Videlicet,[11] a brothel, or so forth.
See you now;
70 Your bait of falsehood takes this carp of truth;
And thus do we of wisdom and of reach,
With windlasses[12] and with assays[13] of bias,†
By indirections find directions out.
So, by my former lecture and advice,
75 Shall you my son. You have me, have you not?
REYNALDO: My lord, I have.
POLONIUS: God be wi' ye. Fare ye well!
REYNALDO: Good my lord!
POLONIUS: Observe his inclination in yourself.
80 REYNALDO: I shall, my lord.
POLONIUS: And let him play his music.
REYNALDO: Well, my lord.
POLONIUS: Farewell!   *Exit Reynaldo.*

Enter Ophelia.
How now, Ophelia, what's the matter?
85 OPHELIA: O, my lord, my lord, I have been so affrighted!
POLONIUS: With what, i' the name of God?
OPHELIA: My lord, as I was sewing in my closet,
Lord Hamlet, with his doublet[14] all unbraced,[15]
No hat upon his head, his stockings fouled,
90 Ungartered,[16] and down-gyved[17] to his ankle;
Pale as his shirt, his knees knocking each other,
And with a look so piteous in purport[18]
As if he had been loosed out of hell
To speak of horrors, he comes before me.
95 POLONIUS: Mad for thy love?
OPHELIA: My lord, I do not know,
But truly I do fear it.
POLONIUS: What said he?
OPHELIA: He took me by the wrist and held me hard;
100 Then goes he to the length of all his arm,
And, with his other hand thus o'er his brow,
He falls to such perusal of my face
As he would draw it. Long stay'd he so.
At last, a little shaking of mine arm,

[11]*for example*

[12]*roundabout trips*†
[13]*attempts*

[14]*jacket*
[15]*unfastened*
[16]*untied*
[17]*hanging down*
[18]*effect*

105 And thrice his head thus waving up and down,
 He raised a sigh so piteous and profound
 As it did seem to shatter all his bulk
 And end his being. That done, he lets me go,
 And with his head over his shoulder turn'd
110 He seem'd to find his way without his eyes;
 For out o' doors he went without their help,
 And to the last bended their light on me.
POLONIUS: Come, go with me. I will go seek the King.
 This is the very ecstasy of love,

[19]*ruins*

115 Whose violent property fordoes[19] itself
 And leads the will to desperate undertakings
 As oft as any passion under heaven
 That does afflict our natures. I am sorry.
 What, have you given him any hard words of late?
120 OPHELIA: No, my good lord; but, as you did command,
 I did repel his letters and denied
 His access to me.
POLONIUS: That hath made him mad.
 I am sorry that with better heed and judgment
125 I had not quoted him. I fear'd he did but trifle
 And meant to wrack thee; but beshrew my jealousy!
 By heaven, it is as proper to our age
 To cast beyond ourselves in our opinions
 As it is common for the younger sort
130 To lack discretion. Come, go we to the King.
 This must be known; which, being kept close, might move
 More grief to hide than hate to utter love.[20]

[20]*i.e., Hamlet's love would cause more hatred if Polonius hid it than if he revealed it.*

             Exeunt.

[SCENE II]
[Elsinore. A room in the Castle.]

[Flourish. Enter King, Queen, Rosencrantz and Guildenstern, and attendants.]

KING: Welcome, dear Rosencrantz and Guildenstern.
    Moreover that we much did long to see you,
    The need we have to use you did provoke
    Our hasty sending. Something have you heard
5   Of Hamlet's transformation—so call it,
    Sith[21] nor the exterior nor the inward man
    Resembles that it was. What it should be,
    More than his father's death, that thus hath put him
    So much from the understanding of himself,
10   I cannot dream of. I entreat you both
    That, being of so young days brought up with him,
    And sith so neighbour'd[22] to his youth and haviour,
    That you vouchsafe your rest here in our court
    Some little time, so by your companies
15   To draw him on to pleasures, and to gather
    So much as from occasion you may glean,
    Whether aught to us unknown afflicts him thus
    That open'd lies within our remedy.
QUEEN: Good gentlemen, he hath much talk'd of you,
20   And sure I am two men there are not living
    To whom he more adheres. If it will please you
    To show us so much gentry and good will
    As to expend your time with us awhile
    For the supply and profit of our hope,
25   Your visitation shall receive such thanks
    As fits a king's remembrance.
ROSENCRANTZ: Both your Majesties
    Might, by the sovereign power you have of us,
    Put your dread pleasures more into command
30   Than to entreaty.
GUILDENSTERN: But we both obey,
    And here give up ourselves, in the full bent,[23]
    To lay our service freely at your feet,
    To be commanded.

[21]*since*

[22]*acquainted*

[23]*extent*

35 KING: Thanks, Rosencrantz and gentle Guildenstern.

QUEEN: Thanks, Guildenstern and gentle Rosencrantz.

And I beseech you instantly to visit

My too much changed son. Go, some of you,

And bring these gentlemen where Hamlet is.

40 GUILDENSTERN: Heavens make our presence and our practices

Pleasant and helpful to him!

QUEEN: Ay, amen!

Exeunt Rosencrantz and Guildenstern.

Enter Polonius.

Sent to find out Why Hamlet went Crazy

POLONIUS: The ambassadors from Norway, my good lord,

Are joyfully return'd.

45 KING: Thou still hast been the father of good news.

POLONIUS: Have I, my lord? Assure you, my good liege,

I hold my duty as I hold my soul,

Both to my God and to my gracious King.

And I do think, or else this brain of mine

50 Hunts not the trail of policy so sure

As it hath used to do, that I have found

The very cause of Hamlet's lunacy.

KING: O, speak of that! That do I long to hear.

POLONIUS: Give first admittance to the ambassadors.

55 My news shall be the fruit to that great feast.

KING: Thyself do grace to them, and bring them in.

                                        [Exit Polonius.]

He tells me, my dear Gertrude, he hath found

The head and source of all your son's distemper.[24]

QUEEN: I doubt it is no other but the main,

60 His father's death and our o'erhasty marriage.

KING: Well, we shall sift him.

Enter [Polonius, Voltimand, and Cornelius, Ambassadors.]

Welcome, my good friends.

Say, Voltimand, what from our brother Norway?

VOLTIMAND: Most fair return of greetings and desires.

65 Upon our first, he sent out to suppress

His nephew's levies; which to him appear'd

[24]*strange behavior*

To be a preparation 'gainst the Polack,
But better look'd into, he truly found
It was against your Highness; whereat griev'd,
70 That so his sickness, age, and impotence
Was falsely borne in hand, sends out arrests
On Fortinbras; which he, in brief, obeys,
Receives rebuke from Norway, and, in fine,[25]
Makes vow before his uncle never more
75 To give the assay[26] of arms against your Majesty.
Whereon old Norway, overcome with joy,
Gives him three thousand crowns[27] in annual fee
And his commission to employ those soldiers,
So levied as before, against the Polack;
80 With an entreaty, herein further shown,
That it might please you to give quiet pass
Through your dominions for this enterprise,
On such regards of safety and allowance
As therein are set down.
85 KING: It likes us well;
And at our more consider'd time we'll read,
Answer, and think upon this business.
Meantime we thank you for your well-took labour.
Go to your rest; at night we'll feast together.
90 Most welcome home! *Exeunt Ambassadors.*
POLONIUS: This business is well ended.
My liege, and madam, to expostulate[28]
What majesty should be, what duty is,
Why day is day, night night, and time is time,
95 Were nothing but to waste night, day, and time.
Therefore, since brevity is the soul of wit
And tediousness the limbs and outward flourishes,
I will be brief. Your noble son is mad.
Mad call I it; for, to define true madness,
100 What is't but to be nothing else but mad?
But let that go.
QUEEN: More matter, with less art.
POLONIUS: Madam, I swear I use no art at all.
That he is mad, 'tis true: 'tis true 'tis pity;
105 And pity 'tis 'tis true—a foolish figure![29]
But farewell it, for I will use no art.

[25]*short*

[26]*attempt*

[27]*coins*

[28]*discuss at length*

[29]*figure of speech*

Mad let us grant him then. And now remains
That we find out the cause of this effect
Or rather say, the cause of this defect,
110   For this effect defective comes by cause.
Thus it remains, and the remainder thus.

[30]*consider*

Perpend.[30]
I have a daughter—have while she is mine—
Who in her duty and obedience, mark,
115   Hath given me this. Now gather, and surmise. *[The Letter.]*

To the celestial, and my soul's idol, the most beautified Ophelia—

That's an ill phrase, a vile phrase; 'beautified' is a vile
phrase.
But you shall hear.   *[Reads.]*

120   Thus in her excellent white bosom, these, &c.

QUEEN: Came this from Hamlet to her?
POLONIUS: Good madam, stay awhile. I will be faithful.
                                              [Reads.] Letter.
Doubt thou the stars are fire;
   Doubt that the sun doth move;
125   Doubt truth to be a liar;
   But never doubt I love.

[31]*i.e., the rhythm of the verse*

O dear Ophelia, I am ill at these numbers;[31] I have not art to reckon
my groans. But that I love thee best, O most best, believe it. Adieu.
Thine evermore, most dear lady, whilst this
machine is to him, Hamlet.

130   This, in obedience, hath my daughter shown me;
And more above, hath his solicitings,
As they fell out by time, by means, and place,
All given to mine ear.
KING: But how hath she
135   Receiv'd his love?
POLONIUS: What do you think of me?
KING: As of a man faithful and honourable.

[32]*gladly*

POLONIUS: I would fain[32] prove so. But what might you think,
When I had seen this hot love on the wing—
140   As I perceiv'd it, I must tell you that,

Before my daughter told me—what might you,
Or my dear Majesty your queen here, think,
If I had play'd the desk or table-book,
Or given my heart a winking, mute and dumb,
145   Or look'd upon this love with idle sight?
What might you think? No, I went round to work
And my young mistress thus I did bespeak:
'Lord Hamlet is a prince, out of thy star.
This must not be.' And then I prescripts[33] gave her,   [33]*orders*
150   That she should lock herself from his resort,
Admit no messengers, receive no tokens.
Which done, she took the fruits of my advice,
And he, repellèd—a short tale to make—
Fell into a sadness, then into a fast,
155   Thence to a watch, thence into a weakness,
Thence to a lightness, and, by this declension,[34]   [34]*decline*
Into the madness wherein now he raves,
And all we mourn for.
KING: Do you think 'tis this?
160   QUEEN: It may be, very like.
POLONIUS: Hath there been such a time—I would fain know
          that—
That I have positively said 'Tis so,'
When it proved otherwise?
165   KING: Not that I know.
POLONIUS: Take this from this, if this be otherwise.
If circumstances lead me, I will find
Where truth is hid, though it were hid indeed
Within the centre.
170   KING: How may we try it further?
POLONIUS: You know, sometimes he walks four hours together
Here in the lobby.
QUEEN: So he does indeed.
POLONIUS: At such a time I'll loose my daughter to him.
175   Be you and I behind an arras[35] then;   [35]*curtain*
Mark the encounter. If he love her not,
And he not from his reason fall'n thereon
Let me be no assistant for a state,
But keep a farm and carters.
180   KING: We will try it.

Enter Hamlet [reading on a book.]

QUEEN: But look where sadly the poor wretch comes reading.

POLONIUS: Away, I do beseech you both, away.

Exeunt King and Queen.

I'll board[36] him presently. O, give me leave.

How does my good Lord Hamlet?

185 HAMLET: Well, God-a-mercy.

POLONIUS: Do you know me, my lord?

HAMLET: Excellent well. You are a fishmonger.[37]

POLONIUS: Not I, my lord.

HAMLET: Then I would you were so honest a man.

190 POLONIUS: Honest, my lord?

HAMLET: Ay, sir. To be honest, as this world goes, is to be one
man picked out of ten thousand.

POLONIUS: That's very true, my lord.

HAMLET: For if the sun breed maggots in a dead dog, being a
195   good kissing carrion[38]—Have you a daughter?

POLONIUS: I have, my lord.

HAMLET: Let her not walk i' th' sun. Conception[39] is a blessing,
but not as your daughter may conceive.[40] Friend, look to't.

POLONIUS: How say you by that? Still harping on my daughter.
200   Yet he knew me not at first. He said I was a fishmonger. He
is far gone. And truly in my youth I suffered much extremity for love, very near this. I'll speak to him again.—What
do you read, my lord?

HAMLET: Words, words, words.

205 POLONIUS: What is the matter, my lord?

HAMLET: Between who?

POLONIUS: I mean, the matter that you read, my lord.

HAMLET: Slanders, sir; for the satirical rogue says here that
old men have grey beards; that their faces are wrinkled;
210   their eyes purging thick amber and plum-tree gum; and
that they have a plentiful lack of wit, together with most
weak hams—all which, sir, though I most powerfully and
potently believe, yet I hold it not honesty to have it thus
set down; for you yourself, sir, shall grow old as I am if, if
215   like a crab, you could go backward.

POLONIUS: Though this be madness, yet there is a method
in't.—

Will you walk out of the air, my lord?

---

[36]*approach*

[37]*Polonius is "fish-
ing" for answers
about Hamlet's
condition*

[38]*dead flesh*

[39]*conception of
children*

[40]*imagine*

pun

*Hamlet
starts
to act
crazy *
Different

HAMLET: Into my grave?

220 POLONIUS: Indeed, that is out of the air. *[Aside.]* How pregnant[41]
sometimes his replies are! a happiness that often madness
hits on, which reason and sanity could not so prosperously
be delivered of. I will leave him and suddenly contrive the
means of meeting between him and my daughter.— My

225 honourable lord, I will most humbly take my leave of you.

HAMLET: You cannot, sir, take from me anything that I will
more willingly part withal—except my life, except my life,
except my life.

POLONIUS: Fare you well, my lord.

230 HAMLET: These tedious old fools!

Enter Guildenstern and Rosencrantz.

POLONIUS: You go to seek the Lord Hamlet. There he is.

ROSENCRANTZ: God save you, sir!

[Exit Polonius.]

GUILDENSTERN: My honoured lord!

ROSENCRANTZ: My most dear lord!

235 HAMLET: My excellent good friends! How dost thou,
Guildenstern? Ah, Rosencrantz! Good lads, how do ye
both?

ROSENCRANTZ: As the indifferent[42] children of the earth.

GUILDENSTERN: Happy, in that we are not over happy.

240 On Fortune's cap we are not the very button.

HAMLET: Nor the soles of her shoe?

ROSENCRANTZ: Neither, my lord.

HAMLET: Then you live about her waist, or in the middle of her
favours?

245 GUILDENSTERN: Faith, her privates we.

HAMLET: In the secret parts of Fortune? O! most true! she is a
strumpet. What's the news?

ROSENCRANTZ: None, my lord, but that the world's grown honest.

HAMLET: Then is doomsday near. But your news is not true. Let

250 me question more in particular. What have you, my good
friends, deserved at the hands of Fortune that she sends you
to prison hither?

GUILDENSTERN: Prison, my lord?

HAMLET: Denmark's a prison.

255 ROSENCRANTZ: Then is the world one.

[41]*heavy with sig-*
nificance

[42]*average*

HAMLET: A goodly one; in which there are many confines, wards, and dungeons, Denmark being one o' the worst.

ROSENCRANTZ: We think not so, my lord.

260 HAMLET: Why, then 'tis none to you; for there is nothing either good or bad but thinking makes it so. To me it is a prison.

ROSENCRANTZ: Why, then your ambition makes it one. 'Tis too narrow for your mind.

HAMLET: O God, I could be bounded in a nutshell and count
265 myself a king of infinite space, were it not that I have bad dreams.

GUILDENSTERN: Which dreams indeed are ambition; for the very substance of the ambitious is merely the shadow of a dream.

270 HAMLET: A dream itself is but a shadow.

ROSENCRANTZ: Truly, and I hold ambition of so airy and light a quality that it is but a shadow's shadow.

HAMLET: Then are our beggars bodies, and our monarchs and outstretched heroes the beggars' shadows. Shall we to the
275 court? For, by my fay,[43] I cannot reason.

ROSENCRANTZ AND GUILDENSTERN: We'll wait upon you.

HAMLET: No such matter! I will not sort[44] you with the rest of my servants; for, to speak to you like an honest man, I am most dreadfully attended. But in the beaten way of friend-
280 ship, what make you at Elsinore?

ROSENCRANTZ: To visit you, my lord; no other occasion.

HAMLET: Beggar that I am, I am even poor in thanks; but I thank you; And sure, dear friends, my thanks are too dear a halfpenny. Were you not sent for? Is it your own
285 inclining? Is it a free visitation? Come, deal justly with me. Come, come! Nay, speak.

GUILDENSTERN: What should we say, my lord?

HAMLET: Why, anything, but to the purpose. You were sent for; and there is a kind of confession in your looks, which
290 your modesties have not craft enough to colour. I know the good King and Queen have sent for you.

ROSENCRANTZ: To what end, my lord?

HAMLET: That you must teach me. But let me conjure you by the rights of our fellowship, by the consonancy of our youth, by
295 the obligation of our ever-preserved love, and by what more dear a better proposer could charge you withal, be even and direct with me, whether you were sent for or no.

[43]faith

[44]classify

He would be OK being stuck in a small prision if it weren't for bad dreams

ROSENCRANTZ: What say you?

300 HAMLET: Nay then, I have an eye of you.—If you love me, hold
not off.

GUILDENSTERN: My lord, we were sent for.

HAMLET: I will tell you why. So shall my anticipation prevent
your discovery, and your secrecy to the King and Queen
305 moult no feather. I have of late—but wherefore I know
not—lost all my mirth, forgone all custom of exercises;
and indeed, it goes so heavily with my disposition that this
goodly frame, the earth, seems to me a sterile promontory;[45]
this most excellent canopy, the air, look you, this brave
310 o'erhanging firmament,[46] this majestical roof fretted[47] with
golden fire, why, it appears no other thing to me than a foul
and pestilent congregation of vapours. What a piece of work
is a man! how noble in reason! how infinite in faculty! in
form and moving how express and admirable! in action how
315 like an angel! in apprehension[48] how like a god! the beauty
of the world, the paragon[49] of animals! And yet to me what
is this quintessence[50] of dust? Man delights not me—no, nor
woman neither, though by your smiling you seem to say so.

ROSENCRANTZ: My lord, there was no such stuff in my thoughts.

320 HAMLET: Why did you laugh then, when I said man delights
not me?

ROSENCRANTZ: To think, my lord, if you delight not in man, what
lenten[51] entertainment the players shall receive from you. We
coted[52] them on the way, and hither are they coming to offer
325 you service.

HAMLET: He that plays the king shall be welcome; his Majesty
shall have tribute of me. The adventurous knight shall use
his foil[53] and target; the lover shall not sigh gratis;[54] the
humorous man shall end his part in peace; the clown shall
330 make those laugh whose lungs are tickle o' the sere;[55] and the
lady shall say her mind freely, or the blank verse[56] shall halt[57]
for't. What players are they?

ROSENCRANTZ: Even those you were wont[58] to take such delight
in, the tragedians of the city.[†]

335 HAMLET: How chances it they travel? Their residence, both in
reputation and profit, was better both ways.

ROSENCRANTZ: I think their inhibition[59] comes by the means of
the late innovation.[60]

[45]*the edge of a rock*

[46]*sky*

[47]*adorned*

[48]*understanding*

[49]*most excellent
example*

[50]*purest form*[†]

[51]*meager*

[52]*passed*

[53]*sword*

[54]*in vain*

[55]*ready to go off*[†]

[56]*unrhymed iambic
pentameter*[†]

[57]*move clumsily*

[58]*accustomed*

[59]*restriction*

[60]*new rules about
acting*

HAMLET: Do they hold the same estimation they did when I
340   was in the city? Are they so followed?

ROSENCRANTZ: No, indeed, are they not.

HAMLET: How comes it? Do they grow rusty?

ROSENCRANTZ: Nay, their endeavour keeps in the wonted pace;
        but there is, sir, an eyrie[61] of children, little eyases,[62] that
345   cry out on the top of question and are most tyrannically
        clapped for't. These are now the fashion, and so berattle
        the common stages—so they call them—that many wear-
        ing rapiers[63] are afraid of goose-quills and dare scarce come
        thither.

350 HAMLET: What, are they children? Who maintains 'em? How
        are they escoted?[64] Will they pursue the quality[65] no longer
        than they can sing? Will they not say afterwards, if they
        should grow themselves to common players—as it is most
        like, if their means are no better—their writers do them
355   wrong to make them exclaim against their own succession?[66]

ROSENCRANTZ: Faith, there has been much to do on both sides;
        and the nation holds it no sin to tarre[67] them to controversy.
        There was, for a while, no money bid for argument[68] unless
        the poet and the player went to cuffs in the question.

360 HAMLET: Is't possible?

GUILDENSTERN: O, there has been much throwing about of
        brains.

HAMLET: Do the boys carry it away?

ROSENCRANTZ: Ay, that they do, my lord, Hercules and his
365   load too.[69]

HAMLET: It is not very strange; for my uncle is King of
        Denmark, and those that would make mows[70] at him while
        my father lived give twenty, forty, fifty, a hundred ducats[71]
        apiece for his picture in little. 'Sblood, there is something
370   in this more than natural, if philosophy could find it out.

                         Flourish [for the Players.]

GUILDENSTERN: There are the players.

HAMLET: Gentlemen, you are welcome to Elsinore. Your
        hands, come! Then appurtenance[72] of welcome is fashion
375   and ceremony. Let me comply with you in this garb, lest
        my extent to the players—which, I tell you, must show
        fairly outwards—should more appear like entertainment
        than yours. You are welcome. But my uncle-father and
        aunt-mother are deceived.

[61]*nest*

[62]*young hawks*

[63]*daggers*

[64]*paid for*

[65]*profession of acting*

[66]*future*

[67]*provoke*

[68]*plays' subject matter*

[69]*a reference to the Globe Theatre*†

[70]*faces*

[71]*gold coin*

[72]*usual accompaniment*

380 GUILDENSTERN: In what, my dear lord?

HAMLET: I am but mad north-north-west. When the wind is southerly I know a hawk from a handsaw.

Enter Polonius.

POLONIUS: Well be with you, gentlemen!

HAMLET: Hark you, Guildenstern, and you too—at each ear a

385   hearer!

That great baby you see there is not yet out of his swaddling clouts.[73]

    [73]*clothes*

ROSENCRANTZ: Happily he's the second time come to them; for they say an old man is twice a child.

390 HAMLET: I will prophesy he comes to tell me of the players. Mark it. You say right, sir; o' Monday morning; 'twas so indeed.

POLONIUS: My lord, I have news to tell you.

HAMLET: My lord, I have news to tell you. When Roscius[74] was

    [74]*the most famous Roman comic actor*

395   an actor in Rome—

POLONIUS: The actors are come hither, my lord.

HAMLET: Buzz, buzz!

POLONIUS: Upon my honour—

HAMLET: Then came each actor on his ass—

400 POLONIUS: The best actors in the world, either for tragedy, comedy, history, pastoral,[75] pastoral-comical, historical-pastoral, tragical-historical, tragical-comical-historical-pastoral; scene individable, or poem unlimited. Seneca[76] cannot be too heavy, nor Plautus[77] too light. For the law of writ and the

    [75]*set in the country*[†]

    [76]*a Roman writer of tragedies*[†]

    [77]*a Roman writer of comedies*[†]

405   liberty, these are the only men.

HAMLET: O Jephthah,[78] judge of Israel, what a treasure hadst thou!   Polonius being Compared

POLONIUS: What treasure had he, my lord?

HAMLET: Why,

    [78]*in the Bible, a judge forced to sacrifice his daughter*[†]

410   'One fair daughter, and no more,
              The which he loved passing well.'[79]

    [79]*from a traditional ballad about Jephthah*

POLONIUS: Still on my daughter.

HAMLET: Am I not i' the right, old Jephthah?

POLONIUS: If you call me Jephthah, my lord, I have a daughter

415   that I love passing well.

HAMLET: Nay, that follows not.

POLONIUS: What follows then, my lord?

HAMLET: Why,

Still makes no sense

> As by lot, God wot,

420 and then, you know,

> It came to pass, as most like it was.—

The first row of the pious chanson[80] will show you more;
for look where my abridgment[81] comes.

Enter [four or five] Players.

You are welcome, masters; welcome, all. I am glad to see
425 thee well. Welcome, good friends. O, my old friend, why,
thy face is valanced[82] since I saw thee last. Com'st' thou
to' beard[83] me in Denmark? What, my young lady and
mistress? By'r lady, your ladyship is nearer to heaven than
when I saw you last by the altitude of a chopine.[84] Pray
430 God, your voice, like a piece of uncurrent[85] gold, be not
cracked within the ring.[86] Masters, you are all welcome.
We'll e'en to't like French falconers, fly at any thing we see.
We'll have a speech straight. Come, give us a taste of your
quality. Come, a passionate speech.

435 PLAYER: What speech, my good lord?

HAMLET: I heard thee speak me a speech once, but it was never
acted; or if it was, not above once; for the play, I remember,
pleased not the million, 'twas caviary[87] to the general; but it
was—as I received it, and others, whose judgments in such
440 matters cried in the top of mine—an excellent play, well
digested[88] in the scenes, set down with as much modesty
as cunning. I remember one said there were no sallets[89]
in the lines to make the matter savoury, nor no matter in
the phrase that might indict[90] the author of affectation; but
445 called it an honest method, as wholesome as sweet, and
by very much more handsome than fine. One speech in't
I chiefly loved; 'twas Æneas' tale to Dido,[91] and thereabout
of it especially where he speaks of Priam's slaughter. If it
live in your memory, begin at this line—let me see, let me
450 see—

[80] *song*

[81] *cutting-off [of speech]*

[82] *covered [with a beard]*

[83] *defy†*

[84] *tall shoe*

[85] *worthless*

[86] *both "edge of a coin" and "sound"*

[87] *caviar (i.e., too refined)*

[88] *arranged*

[89] *tasty (i.e., vulgar) bits*

[90] *make guilty*

[91] *Æneas and Dido are legendary figures described in the Roman poet Virgil's Æneid†*

Back to Poetry

The rugged Pyrrhus,[92] like th' Hyrcanian beast[93]—
'Tis not so; it begins with Pyrrhus—
The rugged Pyrrhus, he whose sable[94] arms,
Black as his purpose, did the night resemble
455 When he lay couched in the ominous horse,[95]
Hath now this dread and black complexion smear'd
With heraldry more dismal. Head to foot
Now is he total gules,[96] horridly trick'd[97]
With blood of fathers, mothers, daughters, sons.
460 Baked and impasted[98] with the parching streets,
That lend a tyrannous and a damned light
To their lord's murder. Roasted in wrath and fire,
And thus o'er-sized with coagulate[99] gore,
With eyes like carbuncles,[100] the hellish Pyrrhus
465 Old grandsire Priam seeks.
So, proceed you.

POLONIUS: 'Fore God, my lord, well spoken, with good accent[101]
and good discretion.[102]

PLAYER: 'Anon[103] he finds him,
470 Striking too short at Greeks. His antique sword,
Rebellious to his arm, lies where it falls,
Repugnant[104] to command. Unequal match'd,
Pyrrhus at Priam drives, in rage strikes wide;
But with the whiff and wind of his fell[105] sword
475 The unnerved father falls. Then senseless Ilium,[106]
Seeming to feel this blow, with flaming top
Stoops to his base, and with a hideous crash
Takes prisoner Pyrrhus' ear. For lo! his sword,
Which was declining on the milky head
480 Of reverend Priam, seem'd i' the air to stick.
So, as a painted tyrant, Pyrrhus stood,
And like a neutral to his will and matter,
Did nothing.
But as we often see, against some storm,
485 A silence in the heavens, the rack[107] stand still,
The bold winds speechless, and the orb[108] below
As hush as death—anon the dreadful thunder
Doth rend[109] the region; so, after Pyrrhus' pause,
Aroused vengeance sets him new a-work;
490 And never did the Cyclops'[110] hammers fall

Sums up the speech

[92]in the Æneid, a young man who kills the elderly king of Troy, Priam†

[93]tiger

[94]black

[95]the Trojan Horse†

[96]red†

[97]decorated

[98]crusted

[99]clotted

[100]red stones

[101]vocal delivery

[102]judgment

[103]soon

[104]disobedient

[105]cruel

[106]Troy

[107]clouds

[108]globe

[109]split

[110]monster who made armor for the gods†

[111]*the Roman god of war*

[112]*strength*

[113]*conference*

[114]*rims*

[115]*roll*

[116]*hub*

[117]*demons in hell*

[118]*Please*

[119]*obscenity*

[120]*the elderly wife of Priam*

[121]*veiled*

[122]*blinding*

[123]*tears*

[124]*cloth*

[125]*crown*

[126]*having given birth to too many children*

[127]*tearful*

[128]*provided for*

[129]*what they should have*

[130]*by God's little body (an oath)*

On Mars's[111] armour, forged for proof[112] eterne,
With less remorse than Pyrrhus' bleeding sword
Now falls on Priam.
Out, out, thou strumpet, Fortune! All you gods,
495   In general synod[113] take away her power;
Break all the spokes and fellies[114] from her wheel,
And bowl[115] the round nave[116] down the hill of heaven,
As low as to the fiends![117]

POLONIUS: This is too long.

500 HAMLET: It shall to the barber's, with your beard. Prithee[118] say
on. He's for a jig or a tale of bawdry,[119] or he sleeps. Say on;
come to Hecuba.[120] *Gives his place to have sexy stuff*

PLAYER: But who, O who, had seen the mobled[121] queen—

HAMLET: 'The mobled queen'?

505 POLONIUS: That's good! 'mobled queen' is good.

PLAYER: Run barefoot up and down, threatening the flames
With bisson[122] rheum;[123] a clout[124] upon that head
Where late the diadem[125] stood, and for a robe,
About her lank and all o'erteemed[126] loins,
510   A blanket, in the alarm of fear caught up— *Long Lines are them acting out*
Who this had seen, with tongue in venom steep'd *what happen*
'Gainst Fortune's state would treason have pronounced. *in Hamlet*
But if the gods themselves did see her then,
When she saw Pyrrhus make malicious sport
515   In mincing with his sword her husband's limbs,
The instant burst of clamour that she made
Unless things mortal move them not at all
Would have made milch[127] the burning eyes of heaven
And passion in the gods.

520 POLONIUS: Look, whether he has not turned his colour, and
has tears in's eyes. Prithee no more!

HAMLET: 'Tis well. I'll have thee speak out the rest of this
soon. Good my lord, will you see the players well
bestow'd?[128] Do you hear? Let them be well used; for they
525   are the abstract and brief chronicles of the time. After
your death you were better have a bad epitaph than their
ill report while you live.

POLONIUS: My lord, I will use them according to their desert.[129]

HAMLET: God's bodykins,[130] man, much better! Use every
530   man after his desert, and who shall 'scape whipping? Use

them after your own honour and dignity. The less they
deserve, the more merit is in your bounty. Take them in.

POLONIUS: Come, sirs.

535 HAMLET: Follow him, friends. We'll hear a play to-morrow.

> *Exeunt Polonius and all the Players, except the FIRST.*

Dost thou hear me, old friend? Can you play 'The Murder of
Gonzago'?

PLAYER: Ay, my lord.

540 HAMLET: We'll ha't tomorrow night. You could, for a need, study
a speech of some dozen or sixteen lines which I would set
down and insert in't, could you not?

PLAYER: Ay, my lord.

HAMLET: Very well. Follow that lord, and look you mock him

545   not. My good friends, I'll leave you till night. You are welcome to Elsinore.

ROSENCRANTZ: Good my lord!

> *Exeunt [Rosencrantz and Guildenstern.]*

HAMLET: Ay, so, God be wi' ye!

550   Now I am alone.

O, what a rogue and peasant slave am I!
Is it not monstrous that this player here,
But in a fiction, in a dream of passion,
Could force his soul so to his own conceit

555   That from her working all his visage wann'd,[131]
Tears in his eyes, distraction in's aspect,
A broken voice, and his whole function suiting
With forms to his conceit? And all for nothing!
For Hecuba!

560   What's Hecuba to him, or he to Hecuba,
That he should weep for her? What would he do,
Had he the motive and the cue for passion
That I have? He would drown the stage with tears
And cleave[132] the general ear with horrid speech;

565   Make mad the guilty and appal the free,
Confound the ignorant, and amaze indeed
The very faculties of eyes and ears.
Yet I,
A dull and muddy-mettled[133] rascal, peak

570   Like John-a-dreams,[134] unpregnant of my cause,
And can say nothing! No, not for a king,
Upon whose property and most dear life

[131] *grew pale*

[132] *split*

[133] *dull-spirited*

[134] *idle dreamer*

[135]head

           A damn'd defeat was made. Am I a coward?
           Who calls me villain? breaks my pate[135] across?
575   Plucks off my beard and blows it in my face?
           Tweaks me by the nose? gives me the lie i' the throat,
           As deep as to the lungs? Who does me this? Ha!

[136]by God's wounds
   (an oath)

           Ha! 'Swounds,[136] I should take it! for it cannot be   *Gods wounds*
           But I am pigeon-liver'd and lack gall[137]

[137]anger

580   To make oppression bitter, or ere this

[138]local

           I should have fatted all the region[138] kites[139]

[139]scavenging birds

           With this slave's offal.[140] Bloody, bawdy villain!

[140]dead flesh

           Remorseless, treacherous, lecherous, kindless villain!
           O, vengeance!   *Apostrophe*

[141]splendid

585   Why, what an ass am I! This is most brave,[141]
           That I, the son of a dear father murder'd,
           Prompted to my revenge by heaven and hell,
           Must, like a whore, unpack my heart with words
           And fall a-cursing like a very drab,

[142]lowly servant

590   A scullion![142] Fie upon't! Foh!   *Saying he's not a man he's eating saddness*
           About, my brain! Hum, I have heard
           That guilty creatures, sitting at a play,
           Have by the very cunning of the scene
           Been struck so to the soul that presently

[143]crimes

595   They have proclaim'd their malefactions;[143]
           For murder, though it have no tongue, will speak
           With most miraculous organ, I'll have these players
           Play something like the murder of my father
           Before mine uncle. I'll observe his looks;

[144]probe

600   I'll tent[144] him to the quick.[145] If he but blench,[146]

[145]core

           I know my course. The spirit that I have seen

[146]grow pale

           May be a devil; and the devil hath power   *Calling his dads Spirit the devil?*
           T' assume a pleasing shape; yea, and perhaps
           Out of my weakness and my melancholy,
605   As he is very potent with such spirits,
           Abuses me to damn me. I'll have grounds
           More relative than this. The play's the thing
           Wherein I'll catch the conscience of the King.

                                                          Exit.

Having players out out what happened to his dad

[ACT III]

[SCENE I]

[Elsinore. A room in the Castle.]

Enter King, Queen, Polonius, Ophelia, Rosencrantz,
Guildenstern, Lords.

Recap

KING: And can you by no drift[1] of conference[2]
    Get from him why he puts on this confusion,
    Grating so harshly all his days of quiet
    With turbulent and dangerous lunacy?
5 ROSENCRANTZ: He does confess he feels himself distracted,
    But from what cause he will by no means speak.
  GUILDENSTERN: Nor do we find him forward[3] to be sounded,[4]
    But with a crafty madness keeps aloof
    When we would bring him on to some confession
10 Of his true state.
  QUEEN: Did he receive you well?
  ROSENCRANTZ: Most like a gentleman.
  GUILDENSTERN: But with much forcing of his disposition.[5]
  ROSENCRANTZ: Niggard[6] of question, but of our demands
15 Most free in his reply.
  QUEEN: Did you assay him
    To any pastime?[7]
  ROSENCRANTZ: Madam, it so fell out that certain players
    We o'erraught[8] on the way. Of these we told him,
20 And there did seem in him a kind of joy
    To hear of it. They are about the court,
    And, as I think, they have already order
    This night to play before him.
  POLONIUS: 'Tis most true;
25 And he beseech'd me to entreat your Majesties
    To hear and see the matter.

[1]*direction*

[2]*conversation*

[3]*ready*

[4]*questioned*

[5]*good manners*

[6]*stingy*

[7]*distracting enter-*
tainment

[8]*overtook*

Saying he wants
the King & Queen to
specifically come to
the play.

61

KING: With all my heart, and it doth much content me
    To hear him so inclin'd.
    Good gentlemen, give him a further edge
30   And drive his purpose on to these delights.
ROSENCRANTZ: We shall, my lord.
                Exeunt Rosencrantz and Guildenstern.

KING: Sweet Gertrude, leave us too;
    For we have closely[9] sent for Hamlet hither,
    That he, as 'twere by accident, may here

35   Affront[10] Ophelia.
    Her father and myself, lawful espials,[11]
    Will so bestow ourselves that, seeing unseen,
    We may of their encounter frankly judge
    And gather by him, as he is behaved,
40   If't be the affliction of his love or no,
    That thus he suffers for.

QUEEN: I shall obey you;
    And for your part, Ophelia, I do wish
    That your good beauties be the happy cause
45   Of Hamlet's wildness. So shall I hope your virtues
    Will bring him to his wonted way again,
    To both your honours.

OPHELIA: Madam, I wish it may.

POLONIUS: Ophelia, walk you here. Gracious, so please you,
50   We will bestow ourselves. Read on this book,
    That show of such an exercise[12] may colour[13]
    Your loneliness. We are oft to blame in this—
    'Tis too much proved—that with devotion's visage
    And pious action we do sugar o'er
55   The Devil himself.

KING: O, 'tis too true!
    How smart a lash that speech doth give my conscience!
    The harlot's cheek, beautied with plastering art,
    Is not more ugly to the thing that helps it
60   Than is my deed to my most painted word.
    O heavy burden!

Enter Hamlet.
POLONIUS: I hear him coming. Let's withdraw, my lord.
                            [Exeunt.]

---

[9]*privately*

[10]*confront*

[11]*spies*

[12]*devotional exercise (indicating that the book is religious in nature)*

[13]*make convincing*

living or not living ~~hamlet ask~~ Hamlet doesn't

HAMLET: To be, or not to be, that is the question: know how people
honorable

   Whether 'tis nobler in the mind to suffer will view him if

65   The slings and arrows of outrageous fortune he kills himself

   Or to take arms against a sea of troubles, "Hamlets more in
his head then actually

   And by opposing end them. To die, to sleep— someone physically

   No more—and by a sleep to say we end killing him

   The heartache, and the thousand natural shocks

70   That flesh is heir to. 'Tis a consummation Parallel Structure
we can end all

   Devoutly to be wish'd. To die, to sleep— pain by putting ourself

   To sleep—perchance to dream. Ay, there's the rub! to sleep

   For in that sleep of death what dreams may come, "There's the catch

   When we have shuffled off this mortal coil,

75   Must give us pause—there's the respect respecting old people

   That makes calamity of so long life. *disaster* pefor living that long

   For who would bear the whips and scorns of time,

   The oppressor's wrong, the proud man's contumely,[14] Sea of [14]*rudeness*
troubles

   The pangs of disprized love, the law's delay,

80   The insolence of office, and the spurns many people

   That patient merit of the unworthy takes, opressing him

   When he himself might his quietus[15] make taken what [15]*end*

   With a bare bodkin?[16] Who would fardels[17] bear, was good [16]*dagger*
turned it bad

   To grunt and sweat under a weary life, [17]*burdens*

85   But that the dread of something after death

   The undiscover'd country, from whose bourn[18] [18]*region*

   No traveller returns, puzzles the will,

   And makes us rather bear those ills we have

   Than fly to others that we know not of? Our iner

90   Thus conscience does make cowards of us all, voice very
judgemental

   And thus the native hue of resolution

   Is sicklied o'er with the pale cast of thought, His indicision

   And enterprises of great pitch[19] and moment very frustated [19]*importance*

   With this regard their currents turn awry

95   And lose the name of action. Soft you now!

   The fair Ophelia! Nymph, in thy orisons[20] Going through [20]*prayers*

   Be all my sins remembered.

OPHELIA: Good my lord, Pros & Cons

   How does your honour for this many a day? of killing

100 HAMLET: I humbly thank you; well, well, well. himself

OPHELIA: My lord, I have remembrances of yours

   That I have longed long to redeliver.

I pray you, now receive them.

HAMLET: No, not I!

105   I never gave you aught.

OPHELIA: My honour'd lord, you know right well you did,
And with them words of so sweet breath compos'd
As made the things more rich. Their perfume lost,
Take these again; for to the noble mind

110   Rich gifts wax poor when givers prove unkind.
There, my lord.

HAMLET: Ha, ha! Are you honest?[21]

OPHELIA: My lord?

HAMLET: Are you fair?

115   OPHELIA: What means your lordship?

HAMLET: That if you be honest and fair, your honesty should admit no discourse to your beauty.

OPHELIA: Could beauty, my lord, have better commerce than with honesty?

120   HAMLET: Ay, truly; for the power of beauty will sooner transform honesty from what it is to a bawd[22] than the force of honesty can translate beauty into his likeness. This was sometime a paradox, but now the time gives it proof. I did love you once.

125   OPHELIA: Indeed, my lord, you made me believe so.

HAMLET: You should not have believed me; for virtue cannot so inoculate[23] our old stock but we shall relish[24] of it. I loved you not.

OPHELIA: I was the more deceived.

130   HAMLET: Get thee to a nunnery! Why wouldst thou be a breeder of sinners? I am myself indifferent honest, but yet I could accuse me of such things that it were better my mother had not borne me. I am very proud, revengeful, ambitious; with more offences at my beck than I have

135   thoughts to put them in, imagination to give them shape, or time to act them in. What should such fellows as I do, crawling between earth and heaven? We are arrant knaves all; believe none of us. Go thy ways to a nunnery. Where's your father?

140   OPHELIA: At home, my lord.

HAMLET: Let the doors be shut upon him, that he may play the fool nowhere but in's own house. Farewell.

Lock your dad inside so you can't get out

[21] *sexually pure*

[22] *obscene thing*

[23] *improve the quality of*

[24] *taste*

OPHELIA: O, help him, you sweet heavens!

HAMLET: If thou dost marry, I'll give thee this plague for thy
145   dowry: be thou as chaste as ice, as pure as snow, thou shalt
    not escape calumny.[25] Get thee to a nunnery. Go, farewell. Or
    if thou wilt needs marry, marry a fool; for wise men know
    well enough what monsters you make of them. To a nun-
    nery, go; and quickly too. Farewell.

[25]*slander*

Sex Club

150 OPHELIA: O heavenly powers, restore him!

HAMLET: I have heard of your paintings too, well enough. God
    hath given you one face, and you make yourselves another.
    You jig,[26] you amble, and you lisp; and nickname God's
    creatures and make your wantonness your ignorance. Go to,
155   I'll no more on't! it hath made me mad. I say, we will have
    no more marriages. Those that are married already—all but
    one—shall live; the rest shall keep as they are. To a nunnery,
    go.   *Exit.*

[26]*walk in an affect-
ed way*

OPHELIA: O, what a noble mind is here o'erthrown!
160   The courtier's, scholar's, soldier's, eye, tongue, sword,
    The expectancy and rose of the fair state,
    The glass of fashion and the mould of form,
    The observed of all observers, quite, quite down!
    And I, of ladies most deject and wretched,
165   That suck'd the honey of his music vows,
    Now see that noble and most sovereign reason,
    Like sweet bells jangled, out of tune and harsh;
    That unmatch'd form and feature of blown youth
    Blasted with ecstasy. O, woe is me,
170   To have seen what I have seen, see what I see!   *Exit.*

Enter King and Polonius.

KING: Love? His affections do not that way tend;
    Nor what he spake, though it lack'd form a little,
    Was not like madness. There's something in his soul
    O'er which his melancholy sits on brood;
175   And I do doubt[27] the hatch and the disclose[28]
    Will be some danger; which for to prevent,
    I have in quick determination
    Thus set it down: he shall with speed to England
    For the demand of our neglected tribute.

[27]*fear*

[28]*revealing*

180   Haply the seas, and countries different,   *Wants to*

        With variable objects shall expel   *Ship Hamlet*

        This something-settled matter in his heart, *Out OF the*

        Whereon his brains still beating puts him thus *Country*

        From fashion of himself. What think you on't?

185 POLONIUS: It shall do well. But yet do I believe

        The origin and commencement of his grief

        Sprung from neglected love. How now, Ophelia?

        You need not tell us what Lord Hamlet said.

        We heard it all. My lord, do as you please;

190   But, if you hold it fit, after the play,

        Let his queen mother all alone entreat him

[29]plain-spoken   To show his grief. Let her be round[29] with him;

        And I'll be placed, so please you, in the ear

        Of all their conference. If she find him not,

195   To England send him; or confine him where

        Your wisdom best shall think.

     KING: It shall be so.

        Madness in great ones must not unwatch'd go.

Exeunt.

[SCENE II]

Hamlet being rude to actors

[Elsinore. A hall in the Castle.]

telling them how to do their job

Enter Hamlet, and three of the Players.

HAMLET: Speak the speech, I pray you, as I pronounced it to
you, trippingly on the tongue. But if you mouth it, as many
[30]rather   of our players do, I had as lief[30] the town-crier spoke my
lines. Nor do not saw the air too much with your hand,
5   thus, but use all gently; for in the very torrent, tempest,
and, as I may say, whirlwind of your passion, you must
acquire and beget a temperance that may give it smooth-
ness. O, it offends me to the soul to hear a robustious[31]
[31]noisy

[32]wig-headed   periwig-pated[32] fellow tear a passion to tatters, to very rags,

10 to split the ears of the groundlings,[33] who, for the most part,
are capable of nothing but inexplicable dumb-shows[34] and
noise. I would have such a fellow whipped for o'erdoing
Termagant.[35] It out-Herods Herod.[36] Pray you avoid it.

FIRST PLAYER: I warrant your honour.

15 HAMLET: Be not too tame neither; but let your own discretion
be your tutor. Suit the action to the word, the word to the
action; with this special observance, that you o'erstep not
the modesty of nature: for anything so overdone is from[37]
the purpose of playing, whose end, both at the first and
20 now, was and is, to hold, as 'twere, the mirror up to nature;
to show virtue her own feature, scorn her own image, and
the very age and body of the time his form and pressure.
Now this overdone, or come tardy off, though it make the
unskilful laugh, cannot but make the judicious grieve; the
25 censure of the which one must in your allowance o'erweigh
a whole theatre of others. O, there be players that I have seen
play, and heard others praise, and that highly, not to speak
it profanely, that, neither having the accent of Christians,
nor the gait of Christian, pagan, nor man, have so strutted
30 and bellowed that I have thought some of Nature's journey-
men[38] had made men, and not made them well, they imitated
humanity so abominably.

FIRST PLAYER: I hope we have reformed that indifferently[39] with
us, sir.

35 HAMLET: O, reform it altogether! And let those that play your
clowns speak no more than is set down for them. For there
be of them that will themselves laugh, to set on some quantity of barren[40] spectators to laugh too, though in the meantime some necessary question of the play be then to be con-
40 sidered. That's villainous and shows a most pitiful ambition
in the fool that uses it. Go make you ready. *[Exit Players.]*

Enter Polonius, Guildenstern, and Rosencrantz.
How now, my lord? Will the King hear this piece of work?

POLONIUS: And the Queen too, and that presently.

HAMLET: Bid the players make haste,　　　　　*[Exit Polonius.]*
45 Will you two help to hasten them?

ROSENCRANTZ AND GUILDENSTERN: We will, my lord.

　　　　　　　　　　　　　　　　　　Exeunt they two.

[33]*lowest class of theater audience*†

[34]*brief pantomimes that introduce a main play*

[35]*a noisy god in early plays*†

[36]*The character of Herod was associated with ranting and raving.*†

[37]*contrary to*

[38]*amateur craftsmen*

[39]*fairly well*

[40]*unmoved*

HAMLET: What, ho, Horatio!

Enter Horatio.

HORATIO: Here, sweet lord, at your service.
HAMLET: Horatio, thou art e'en as just a man
50   As e'er my conversation cop'd withal.
HORATIO: O, my dear lord!
HAMLET: Nay, do not think I flatter;
         For what advancement may I hope from thee,
         That no revenue[41] hast but thy good spirits
55   To feed and clothe thee? Why should the poor be flatter'd?
         No, let the candied tongue lick absurd pomp,
         And crook the pregnant[42] hinges of the knee
         Where thrift[43] may follow fawning.[44] Dost thou hear?
         Since my dear soul was mistress of her choice,
60   And could of men distinguish her election,
         Sh'hath seal'd thee for herself. For thou hast been
         As one, in suff'ring all, that suffers nothing;
         A man that Fortune's buffets[45] and rewards
         Hast ta'en with equal thanks; and blest are those
65   Whose blood and judgment are so well commeddled[46]
         That they are not a pipe for Fortune's finger
         To sound[47] what stop[48] she please. Give me that man
         That is not passion's slave, and I will wear him
         In my heart's core, ay, in my heart of heart,
70   As I do thee. Something too much of this.
         There is a play tonight before the King.
         One scene of it comes near the circumstance,
         Which I have told thee, of my father's death.
         I prithee, when thou seest that act afoot,
75   Even with the very comment of thy soul
         Observe my uncle. If his occulted[49] guilt
         Do not itself unkennel[50] in one speech,
         It is a damned ghost that we have seen,
         And my imaginations are as foul
80   As Vulcan's[51] stithy.[52] Give him heedful note;
         For I mine eyes will rivet to his face,
         And after we will both our judgments join
         In censure of his seeming.

[41]*earthly possessions*

[42]*quick to kneel*

[43]*profit*

[44]*flattery*

[45]*hits*

[46]*mixed together*

[47]*play*

[48]*note*

[49]*hidden*

[50]*let loose*

[51]*the god of metal-working*

[52]*forge*†

85 HORATIO: Well, my lord.
    If he steal aught the whilst this play is playing,
    And 'scape detecting, I will pay the theft.

                                          [Sound a flourish.]

    HAMLET: They are coming to the play. I must be idle.
    Get you a place.

[Danish march. Enter Trumpets and Kettle Drums. Enter King,
Queen, Polonius, Ophelia, Rosencrantz, Guildenstern, and other
Lords attendant, with the Guard carrying torches.]

90 KING: How fares[53] our cousin Hamlet?
    HAMLET: Excellent, i' faith; of the chameleon's[54] dish. I eat the
      air, promise-cramm'd. You cannot feed capons[55] so.
    KING: I have nothing with this answer, Hamlet. These words
      are not mine.
95 HAMLET: No, nor mine now. My lord, you play'd once i' th' uni-
      versity, you say?
    POLONIUS: That did I, my lord, and was accounted a good actor.
    HAMLET: What did you enact?
    POLONIUS: I did enact Julius Caesar; I was killed i' the Capitol;
100   Brutus killed me.
    HAMLET: It was a brute part of him to kill so capital a calf there.
      Be the players ready.
    ROSENCRANTZ: Ay, my lord. They stay upon your patience.
    QUEEN: Come hither, my dear Hamlet, sit by me.
105 HAMLET: No, good mother. Here's metal more attractive.
    POLONIUS: O, ho! do you mark that?
    HAMLET: Lady, shall I lie in your lap?   *Flirting with Ophelia*
    OPHELIA: No, my lord.
    HAMLET: I mean, my head upon your lap?
110 OPHELIA: Ay, my lord.
    HAMLET: Do you think I meant country[56] matters?
    OPHELIA: I think nothing, my lord.
    HAMLET: That's a fair thought to lie between maids' legs.
    OPHELIA: What is, my lord?
115 HAMLET: Nothing.
    OPHELIA: You are merry, my lord.
    HAMLET: Who, I?

[53]The king uses
fare *to mean
"feel," but Hamlet
takes its second
meaning, "to eat."*

[54]*Chameleons were
said to eat air.*

[55]*chickens*

[56]*sexual*

[57] *writer of upbeat dances*

OPHELIA:　Ay, my lord.

HAMLET:　O God, your only jig-maker![57] What should a man
120　　do but be merry? For, look you, how cheerfully my mother
　　　looks, and my father died within's two hours. *Opposite of*
OPHELIA:　Nay 'tis twice two months, my lord. *hyperbole*

HAMLET:　So long? Nay then, let the devil wear black, for I'll
　　　have a suit of sables.[58] O heavens! die two months ago, and
125　　not forgotten yet? Then there's hope a great man's memory
　　　may outlive his life half a year. But, by'r lady, he must build
　　　churches then; or else shall he suffer not thinking on, with
　　　the hobby-horse,[59] whose epitaph is, 'For, O, for O, the
　　　hobby-horse is forgot!'

[58] *luxurious black furs*

[59] *figure in traditional May dances*

[60] *trumpets*

*[Hautboys[60] play. The dumb-show enters. Enter a King and a
Queen very lovingly; the Queen embracing him and he her. She
kneels, and makes show of protestation unto him. He takes her
up, and declines his head upon her neck. He lays him down upon
a bank of flowers. She, seeing him asleep, leaves him. Anon
comes in a fellow, takes off his crown, kisses it, pours poison
in the King's ears, and leaves him. The Queen returns, finds
the King dead, and makes passionate action. The Poisoner with
some three or four Mutes, comes in again, seeming to lament
with her. The dead body is carried away. The Poisoner woos the
Queen with gifts; she seems loath and unwilling awhile, but in
the end accepts his love.　Exeunt.]*

[61] *sneaking*

[62] *wickedness*

[63] *probably*

[64] *indicates*

130　OPHELIA:　What means this, my lord?
HAMLET:　Marry, this is miching[61] mallecho;[62] it means mischief.
OPHELIA:　Belike[63] this show imports[64] the argument of the play.

Enter Prologue.

HAMLET:　We shall know by this fellow. The players cannot
　　　keep counsel; they'll tell all.
135　OPHELIA:　Will he tell us what this show meant?
HAMLET:　Ay, or any show that you'll show him. Be not you
　　　ashamed to show, he'll not shame to tell you what it means.
OPHELIA:　You are naught, you are naught! I'll mark the play.
PROLOGUE:　For us, and for our tragedy,
140　　Here stooping to your clemency,[65]
　　　We beg your hearing patiently.

[65] *mercy*

HAMLET: Is this a prologue, or the posy[66] of a ring?
OPHELIA: 'Tis brief, my lord.
HAMLET: As woman's love.

Enter [two Players as] King and Queen

145 P. KING: Full thirty times hath Phoebus'[67] cart gone round
　　　　　Neptune's[68] salt wash and Tellus'[69] orbed ground,
　　　　　And thirty dozen moons with borrowed sheen
　　　　　About the world have times twelve thirties been,
　　　　　Since love our hearts, and Hymen[70] did our hands,
150　　　Unite commutual in most sacred bands.
　　　P. QUEEN: So many journeys may the sun and moon
　　　　　Make us again count o'er ere love be done!
　　　　　But woe is me! you are so sick of late,
　　　　　So far from cheer and from your former state.
155　　　That I distrust you. Yet, though I distrust,
　　　　　Discomfort you, my lord, it nothing must;
　　　　　For women's fear and love hold[71] quantity,
　　　　　In neither aught, or in extremity.
　　　　　Now, what my love is, proof hath made you know;
160　　　And as my love is sized, my fear is so.
　　　　　Where love is great, the littlest doubts are fear;
　　　　　Where little fears grow great, great love grows there.
　　　P. KING: Faith, I must leave thee, love, and shortly too;
　　　　　My operant[72] powers their functions leave to do.
165　　　And thou shalt live in this fair world behind,
　　　　　Honour'd, belov'd, and haply one as kind
　　　　　For husband shalt thou—
　　　P. QUEEN: O, confound the rest!
　　　　　Such love must needs be treason in my breast.
170　　　In second husband let me be accurst!
　　　　　None wed the second but who killed the first.
　　　HAMLET: Wormwood, wormwood.
　　　P. QUEEN: The instances[73] that second marriage move
　　　　　Are base[74] respects[75] of thrift,[76] but none of love.
175　　　A second time I kill my husband dead
　　　　　When second husband kisses me in bed.
　　　P. KING: I do believe you think what now you speak;
　　　　　But what we do determine oft we break.
　　　　　Purpose is but the slave to memory,

[66]*poem inscribed inside*

[67]*the god of the sun*

[68]*the god of the sea*

[69]*the Roman goddess of the earth*

[70]*the goddess of marriage*

[71]*have the same*

[72]*vital*

[73]*impulses*

[74]*low, crude*

[75]*considerations*

[76]*money*

180 Of violent birth, but poor validity;
Which now, like fruit unripe, sticks on the tree,
But fall unshaken when they mellow[77] be.
Most necessary 'tis that we forget
To pay ourselves what to ourselves is debt.
185 What to ourselves in passion we propose,
The passion ending, doth the purpose lose.
The violence of either grief or joy
Their own enactures[78] with themselves destroy.
Where joy most revels, grief doth most lament;
190 Grief joys, joy grieves, on slender accident.
This world is not for aye, nor 'tis not strange
That even our loves should with our fortunes change;
For 'tis a question left us yet to prove,
Whether love lead fortune, or else fortune love.
195 The great man down, you mark his favorite flies,
The poor advanced makes friends of enemies;
And hitherto doth love on fortune tend,
For who not needs shall never lack a friend,
And who in want a hollow friend doth try,
200 Directly seasons[79] him his enemy.
But, orderly to end where I begun,
Our wills and fates do so contrary run
That our devices still are overthrown;
Our thoughts are ours, their ends none of our own.
205 So think thou wilt no second husband wed;
But die thy thoughts when thy first lord is dead.
P. QUEEN: Nor earth to me give food, nor heaven light,
Sport and repose lock from me day and night,
To desperation turn my trust and hope,
210 An anchor's[80] cheer in prison be my scope,
Each opposite, that blanks the face of joy,
Meet what I would have well, and it destroy,
Both here and hence pursue me lasting strife,
If, once a widow, ever I be wife!
215 HAMLET: If she should break it now!
P. KING: 'Tis deeply sworn. Sweet, leave me here awhile.
My spirits grow dull, and fain I would beguile
The tedious day with sleep.   *Sleeps.*
P. QUEEN: Sleep rock thy brain,

[77] *ripe*

[78] *fulfillments*

[79] *makes*

[80] *hermit's*

220 And never come mischance between us twain![81] *Exeunt.*

HAMLET: Madam, how like you this play?

QUEEN: The lady doth protest too much, methinks.

HAMLET: O, but she'll keep her word.

KING: Have you heard the argument? Is there no offence in't?

225 HAMLET: No, no! They do but jest, poison in jest; no offence i'
the world.

KING: What do you call the play?

HAMLET: *The Mousetrap.* Marry,[82] how? Tropically.[83] This play is
the image of a murder done in Vienna. Gonzago is the Duke's

230 name; his wife, Baptista. You shall see anon. 'Tis a knavish
piece of work; but what o' that? Your Majesty, and we that
have free[84] souls, it touches us not. Let the galled[85] jade[86]
winch;[87] our withers[88] are unwrung.[89]

This is one Lucianus, nephew to the King.

Enter Lucianus.

235 OPHELIA: You are as good as a chorus, my lord.

HAMLET: I could interpret between you and your love, if I could
see the puppets[90] dallying.

OPHELIA: You are keen,[91] my lord, you are keen.

HAMLET: It would cost you a groaning to take off my edge.

240 OPHELIA: Still better, and worse.

HAMLET: So you must take your husbands. Begin, murderer.
Pox, leave thy damnable faces, and begin! Come, the croak-
ing raven doth bellow for revenge.

LUCIANUS: Thoughts black, hands apt, drugs fit, and time

245 agreeing;
Confederate[92] season, else no creature seeing;
Thou mixture rank, of midnight weeds collected,
With Hecate's[93] ban[94] thrice blasted, thrice infected,
Thy natural magic and dire property

250 On wholesome life usurp immediately.

[Pours the poison in his ears.]

HAMLET: He poisons him i' the garden for his estate. His name's
Gonzago. The story is extant, and written in very choice
Italian. You shall see anon how the murderer gets the love
of Gonzago's wife.

255 OPHELIA: The King rises.

HAMLET: What, frighted with false fire?

---

[81] *two*

[82] *by the Virgin Mary (an oath)*

[83] *as a trope (figure of speech)*

[84] *innocent*

[85] *sore*

[86] *old horse*

[87] *wince*

[88] *shoulders*

[89] *not rubbed raw*

[90] *Hamlet imagines Ophelia and her lover as puppets.*

[91] *cutting*

[92] *cooperating*

[93] *the goddess of dark magic*†

[94] *curse*

QUEEN: How fares my lord?

POLONIUS: Give o'er the play.

KING: Give me some light. Away!

260 ALL: Lights, lights, lights!

Exeunt all but Hamlet and Horatio.

HAMLET: Why, let the stricken deer go weep,
                        The hart[95] ungalled play;
                        For some must watch, while some must sleep:
                        Thus runs the world away.

[handwritten: Singing Hamlet bc he's so happy]

95 *deer*

96 *Feathers were often worn on actors' hats.*

97 *decorative fabric roses*

98 *decorated*

99 *partnership*

100 *company*

265   Would not this, sir, and a forest of feathers[96]—if the rest of my fortunes turn Turk with me—with two Provincial roses[97] on my razed[98] shoes, get me a fellowship[99] in a cry[100] of players, sir?

HORATIO: Half a share.

270 HAMLET: A whole one, I!

                        For thou dost know, O Damon dear,
                        This realm dismantled[101] was
                        Of Jove[102] himself; and now reigns here
                        A very, very—pajock.[103]

101 *stripped*

102 *the king of the gods*

103 *peacock*

275 HORATIO: You might have rhymed.

HAMLET: O good Horatio, I'll take the ghost's word for a
               thousand pound!
         Didst perceive?

HORATIO: Very well, my lord.

280 HAMLET: Upon the talk of the poisoning?

HORATIO: I did very well note him.

HAMLET: Ah, ha! Come, some music! Come, the recorders!

                        For if the King like not the comedy,
                        Why then, belike, he likes it not, perdy.[104]

104 *by God*

285   Come, some music!

Enter Rosencrantz and Guildenstern.

GUILDENSTERN: Good my lord, vouchsafe me a word with you.

HAMLET: Sir, a whole history.

GUILDENSTERN: The King, sir—

HAMLET:　Ay, sir, what of him?

290　GUILDENSTERN:　Is in his retirement,[105] marvellous distempered.

HAMLET:　With drink, sir?

GUILDENSTERN:　No, my lord; rather with choler.[106]

HAMLET:　Your wisdom should show itself more richer to signify this to the doctor; for, for me to put him to his purgation[107]

295　would perhaps plunge him into far more choler.

GUILDENSTERN:　Good my lord, put your discourse into some frame,[108] and start not so wildly from my affair.

HAMLET:　I am tame, sir. Pronounce.

GUILDENSTERN:　The Queen, your mother, in most great affliction

300　of spirit hath sent me to you.

HAMLET:　You are welcome.

GUILDENSTERN:　Nay, good my lord, this courtesy is not of the right breed. If it shall please you to make me a wholesome answer, I will do your mother's commandment; if not, your

305　pardon and my return shall be the end of my business.

HAMLET:　Sir, I cannot.

GUILDENSTERN:　What, my lord?

HAMLET:　Make you a wholesome answer. My wit's diseased. But, sir, such answer as I can make, you shall command; or

310　rather, as you say, my mother. Therefore no more, but to the matter! My mother, you say—

ROSENCRANTZ:　Then thus she says: your behaviour hath struck her into amazement and admiration.

HAMLET:　O wonderful son, that can so astonish a mother! But

315　is there no sequel[109] at the heels of this mother's admiration? Impart.

ROSENCRANTZ:　She desires to speak with you in her closet, ere you go to bed.

HAMLET:　We shall obey, were she ten times our mother. Have

320　you any further trade with us?

ROSENCRANTZ:　My lord, you once did love me.

HAMLET:　So I do still, by these pickers and stealers![110]

ROSENCRANTZ:　Good my lord, what is your cause of distemper? You do surely bar the door upon your own liberty, if you

325　deny your griefs to your friend.

HAMLET:　Sir, I lack advancement.

ROSENCRANTZ:　How can that be, when you have the voice of the King himself for your succession in Denmark?

[105] *rest*

[106] *anger*

[107] *bodily cleansing*†

[108] *order*

[109] *further subject matter*

[110] *hands*

She sent you just to compliment me?

Enter the Players with recorders.

[111]*a proverb that ends, "the horse starves"*

[112]*get on my windward side, like a hunter*

[113]*trap*

[114]*openings*

[115]*range*

[116]*God's blood (an oath)*

HAMLET: Ay, sir, but 'while the grass grows'[111]—the proverb is
330   something musty.
       O, the recorders! Let me see one. To withdraw with you—
       why do you go about to recover the wind[112] of me, as if you
       would drive me into a toil?[113]

GUILDENSTERN: O, my lord, if my duty be too bold, my love is
335   too unmannerly.

HAMLET: I do not well understand that. Will you play upon
       this pipe?

GUILDENSTERN: My lord, I cannot.

HAMLET: I pray you.

340 GUILDENSTERN: Believe me, I cannot.

HAMLET: I do beseech you.

GUILDENSTERN: I know no touch of it, my lord.

HAMLET: It is as easy as lying. Govern these ventages[114] with
       your fingers and thumbs, give it breath with your mouth,
345   and it will discourse most eloquent music. Look you, these
       are the stops.

GUILDENSTERN: But these cannot I command to any utterance
       of harmony. I have not the skill.

HAMLET: Why, look you now, how unworthy a thing you
350   make of me! You would play upon me; you would seem to
       know my stops; you would pluck out the heart of my mys-
       tery; you would sound me from my lowest note to the top
       of my compass;[115] and there is much music, excellent voice,
       in this little organ, yet cannot you make it speak. 'Sblood,[116]
355   do you think I am easier to be played on than a pipe? Call
       me what instrument you will, though you can fret me, you
       cannot play upon me.
       God bless you, sir!

Enter Polonius.   Long sex joke

POLONIUS: My lord, the Queen would speak with you, and
360   presently.

HAMLET: Do you see yonder cloud that's almost in shape of a
       camel?

POLONIUS: By the mass, and 'tis like a camel, indeed.

HAMLET: Methinks it is like a weasel.
365 POLONIUS: It is backed like a weasel.
HAMLET: Or like a whale.
POLONIUS: Very like a whale.
HAMLET: Then will I come to my mother by and by. They fool
me to the top of my bent.—I will come by and by.
370 POLONIUS: I will say so.   *[Exit.]*
HAMLET: 'By and by' is easily said. Leave me, friends.
                         [Exeunt all but Hamlet.]
'Tis now the very witching time of night,
When churchyards yawn, and hell itself breathes out
Contagion to this world. Now could I drink hot blood,
375 And do such bitter business as the day
Would quake to look on. Soft! now to my mother!
O heart, lose not thy nature; let not ever
The soul of Nero[117] enter this firm bosom.
Let me be cruel, not unnatural;
380 I will speak daggers to her, but use none.
My tongue and soul in this be hypocrites
How in my words soever she be shent,[118]
To give them seals never, my soul, consent![119]

                                   Exit.

[SCENE III]
[Elsinore.]

[Enter King, Rosencrantz, and Guildenstern.]

KING: I like him not, nor stands it safe with us
To let his madness range.[120] Therefore prepare you.
I your commission[121] will forthwith dispatch,[122]
And he to England shall along with you.
5 The terms of our estate may not endure
Hazard so near us as doth hourly grow
Out of his brows.
GUILDENSTERN: We will ourselves provide.
Most holy and religious fear it is
10 To keep those many many bodies safe
That live and feed upon your Majesty.
ROSENCRANTZ: The single and peculiar life is bound

[117]*the Roman emperor who killed his mother*

[118]*criticized*

[119]*(i.e., Do not allow my words to be followed up with violent action.)*

[120]*roam freely about*

[121]*task*

[122]*set in motion*

With all the strength and armour of the mind
To keep itself from noyance; but much more

15 That spirit upon whose weal[123] depends and rests
The lives of many. The cess[124] of majesty
Dies not alone, but like a gulf doth draw
What's near it with it. It is a massy wheel,
Fix'd on the summit of the highest mount,

20 To whose huge spokes ten thousand lesser things *talking about*
Are mortised[125] and adjoin'd; which, when it falls, *Planet*
Each small annexment,[126] petty consequence,
Attends the boisterous ruin. Never alone
Did the King sigh, but with a general groan. *Metaphor*

25 KING: Arm you, I pray you, to this speedy voyage;
For we will fetters[127] put upon this fear,
Which now goes too free-footed.

ROSENCRANTZ AND GUILDENSTERN: We will haste us.
Saying however the king Exeunt Gentlemen.
feels everyone feels.

Enter Polonius.

POLONIUS: My lord, he's going to his mother's closet.[128]

30 Behind the arras I'll convey myself,
To hear the process. I'll warrant she'll tax[129] him home;
And, as you said, and wisely was it said,
'Tis meet that some more audience than a mother,
Since nature makes them partial, should o'erhear

35 The speech, of vantage. Fare you well, my liege.
I'll call upon you ere you go to bed
And tell you what I know.   Exit [Polonius.]

KING: Thanks, dear my lord.
O, my offence is rank, it smells to heaven;

40 It hath the primal[130] eldest curse upon't,
A brother's murder! Pray can I not,
Though inclination be as sharp as will;
My stronger guilt defeats my strong intent,
And, like a man to double business bound,

45 I stand in pause where I shall first begin,
And both neglect. What if this cursed hand
Were thicker than itself with brother's blood,
Is there not rain enough in the sweet heavens

123 *well-being*
124 *decease*
125 *cemented*
126 *attachment*
127 *shackles*
128 *chamber*
129 *scold*
130 *first*†

To wash it white as snow? Whereto serves mercy
50   But to confront the visage of offence?
And what's in prayer but this twofold force,
To be forestalled[131] ere we come to fall,
Or pardon'd being down? Then I'll look up;
My fault is past. But, O, what form of prayer
55   Can serve my turn? 'Forgive me my foul murder?'
That cannot be; since I am still possess'd
Of those effects[132] for which I did the murder—
My crown, mine own ambition, and my queen.
May one be pardon'd and retain the offence?
60   In the corrupted currents of this world
Offence's gilded[133] hand may shove by justice,
And oft 'tis seen the wicked prize itself
Buys out the law; but 'tis not so above:
There is no shuffling; there the action lies
65   In his true nature, and we ourselves compell'd,
Even to the teeth and forehead of our faults,
To give in evidence. What then? What rests?
Try what repentance can. What can it not?
Yet what can it when one cannot repent?
70   O wretched state! O bosom black as death!
O limed[134] soul, that, struggling to be free,
Art more engaged! Help, angels! Make assay.
Bow, stubborn knees; and heart with strings of steel,
Be soft as sinews of the new-born babe!
75   All may be well.   *[He kneels.]*

Enter Hamlet.

HAMLET: Now might I do it pat,[135] now he is praying;
And now I'll do't. And so he goes to heaven,
And so am I revenged. That would[136] be scann'd.[137]
A villain kills my father; and for that,
80   I, his sole son, do this same villain send
To heaven.
O, this is hire and salary, not revenge!
He took my father grossly, full of bread,
With all his crimes broad blown, as flush as May;
85   And how his audit[138] stands, who knows save heaven?

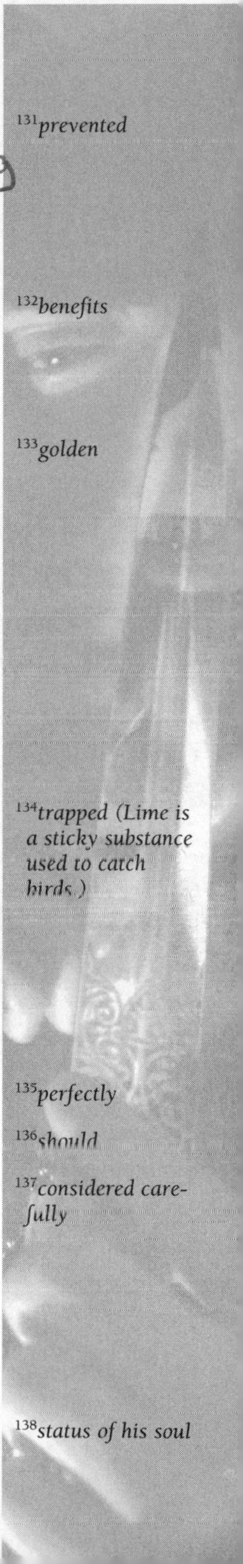

Praying [handwritten annotation]

[131]*prevented*

[132]*benefits*

[133]*golden*

[134]*trapped (Lime is a sticky substance used to catch birds.)*

[135]*perfectly*

[136]*should*

[137]*considered carefully*

[138]*status of his soul*

But in our circumstance and course of thought,
'Tis heavy with him; and am I then revenged,
To take him in the purging of his soul,
When he is fit and seasoned for his passage?

90 No.

[139] *grasping*[†]

Up, sword, and know thou a more horrid hent.[139]
When he is drunk asleep; or in his rage;
Or in the incestuous pleasure of his bed;
At game, a-swearing, or about some act

95 That has no relish of salvation in't
Then trip him, that his heels may kick at heaven,
And that his soul may be as damn'd and black
As hell, whereto it goes. My mother stays.

[140] *medicine*

This physic[140] but prolongs thy sickly days.   *Exit.*

100 KING: My words fly up, my thoughts remain below.
Words without thoughts never to heaven go.

                                        Exit.

[SCENE IV]
[The Queen's closet.]

Enter [Queen] Gertrude and Polonius.

[141] *immediately*

POLONIUS: He will come straight.[141] Look you lay home to him.
Tell him his pranks have been too broad to bear with,
And that your Grace hath screen'd and stood between

[142] *anger*

Much heat[142] and him. I'll silence me even here.

5 Pray you, be round with him.
QUEEN: I'll warrant you;
Fear me not. Withdraw; I hear him coming.
           [Polonius hides behind the arras.]

Enter Hamlet.

HAMLET: Now, mother, what's the matter?
QUEEN: Hamlet, thou hast thy father much offended.
10 HAMLET: Mother, you have my father much offended.

QUEEN: Come, come, you answer with an idle tongue.

HAMLET: Go, go, you question with a wicked tongue.

QUEEN: Why, how now, Hamlet?

HAMLET: What's the matter now?

15 QUEEN: Have you forgot me?

HAMLET: No, by the rood,[143] not so!

    You are the Queen, your husband's brother's wife,

    And—would it were not so—you are my mother.

QUEEN: Nay, then, I'll set those to you that can speak.

20 HAMLET: Come, come, and sit you down. You shall not budge.

    You go not till I set you up a glass

    Where you may see the inmost part of you.

QUEEN: What wilt thou do? Thou wilt not murder me?

    Help, help, ho!

25 POLONIUS: What, ho! Help, help, help!

HAMLET: How now, a rat? *[Draws.]* Dead for a ducat, dead!

POLONIUS: O, I am slain!   *[Falls and dies.]*

QUEEN: O me, what hast thou done?

HAMLET: Nay, I know not. Is it the King?

30 QUEEN: O, what a rash and bloody deed is this!

HAMLET: A bloody deed. Almost as bad, good mother,

    As kill a king, and marry with his brother.

QUEEN: As kill a king?

HAMLET: Ay, lady, 'twas my word.

35   Thou wretched, rash, intruding fool, farewell!

    I took thee for thy better. Take thy fortune.

    Thou find'st to be too busy is some danger.

    Leave wringing of your hands. Peace! sit you down,

    And let me wring your heart; for so I shall,

40   If it be made of penetrable stuff;

    If damned custom have not braz'd[144] it so

    That it be proof and bulwark against sense.

QUEEN: What have I done, that thou darest wag thy tongue

    In noise so rude against me?

45 HAMLET: Such an act

    That blurs the grace and blush of modesty;

    Calls virtue hypocrite; takes off the rose

    From the fair forehead of an innocent love,

    And sets a blister there; makes marriage vows

50   As false as dicers'[145] oaths—O, such a deed

[143]*cross*

[144]*hardened*

[145]*gamblers'*

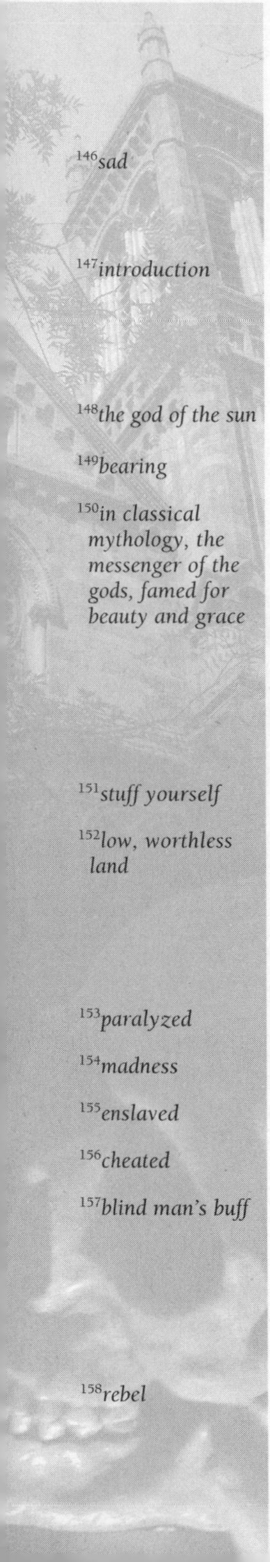

As from the body of contraction plucks
The very soul, and sweet religion makes
A rhapsody of words! Heaven's face doth glow;
Yea, this solidity and compound mass,
55   With tristful[146] visage, as against the doom,
Is thought-sick at the act.

QUEEN: Ay me, what act,
That roars so loud and thunders in the index?[147]

HAMLET: Look here upon this picture, and on this,
60   The counterfeit presentment of two brothers.
See what a grace was seated on this brow;
Hyperion's[148] curls; the front of Jove himself;
An eye like Mars, to threaten and command;
A station[149] like the herald Mercury[150]
65   New lighted on a heaven-kissing hill:
A combination and a form indeed
Where every god did seem to set his seal
To give the world assurance of a man.
This was your husband. Look you now what follows.
70   Here is your husband, like a mildew'd ear
Blasting his wholesome brother. Have you eyes?
Could you on this fair mountain leave to feed,
And batten[151] on this moor?[152] Ha! have you eyes?
You cannot call it love; for at your age
75   The heyday in the blood is tame, it's humble,
And waits upon the judgment; and what judgment
Would step from this to this? Sense sure you have,
Else could you not have motion; but sure that sense
Is apoplex'd;[153] for madness would not err,
80   Nor sense to ecstacy[154] was ne'er so thrall'd[155]
But it reserv'd some quantity of choice
To serve in such a difference. What devil was't
That thus hath cozen'd[156] you at hoodman-blind?[157]
Eyes without feeling, feeling without sight,
85   Ears without hands or eyes, smelling sans all,
Or but a sickly part of one true sense
Could not so mope.
O shame! where is thy blush? Rebellious hell,
If thou canst mutine[158] in a matron's bones,
90   To flaming youth let virtue be as wax

Marginal notes:

[146]sad

[147]introduction

[148]the god of the sun

[149]bearing

[150]in classical mythology, the messenger of the gods, famed for beauty and grace

[151]stuff yourself

[152]low, worthless land

[153]paralyzed

[154]madness

[155]enslaved

[156]cheated

[157]blind man's buff

[158]rebel

Handwritten annotations:

Why would you go from daddy h to uncle C?

How could you go from Hamlet to Claudius?

And melt in her own fire. Proclaim no shame
When the compulsive ardour gives the charge,
Since frost itself as actively doth burn,
And reason panders[159] will.

95   QUEEN: O Hamlet, speak no more!
Thou turn'st mine eyes into my very soul,
And there I see such black and grained spots
As will not leave their tinct.[160]

HAMLET: Nay, but to live
100   In the rank sweat of an enseamed[161] bed,
Stew'd in corruption, honeying and making love
Over the nasty sty![162]

QUEEN: O, speak to me no more!
These words like daggers enter in mine ears.
105   No more, sweet Hamlet!

HAMLET: A murderer and a villain!
A slave that is not twentieth part the tithe[163]
Of your precedent lord; a vice of kings;
A cutpurse[164] of the empire and the rule,
110   That from a shelf the precious diadem stole
And put it in his pocket!

QUEEN: No more!

Enter the Ghost

HAMLET: A king of shreds and patches—
Save me and hover o'er me with your wings,
115   You heavenly guards! What would your gracious figure?

QUEEN: Alas, he's mad!

HAMLET: Do you not come your tardy son to chide,
That, lapsed in time and passion, lets go by
The important acting of your dread command?
120   O, say!

GHOST: Do not forget. This visitation
Is but to whet[165] thy almost blunted purpose.
But look, amazement on thy mother sits.
O, step between her and her fighting soul!
125   Conceit in weakest bodies strongest works.
Speak to her, Hamlet.

HAMLET: How is it with you, lady?

[159]*does the bidding of*

[160]*color*

[161]*greasy*

[162]*pigsty*

[163]*a 10% portion*

[164]*pickpocket*

[165]*sharpen*

[166]*formless*

QUEEN: Alas, how is't with you,
> That you do bend your eye on vacancy,
130   And with the incorporal[166] air do hold discourse?
> Forth at your eyes your spirits wildly peep;
> And, as the sleeping soldiers in the alarm,

[167]*outgrowths*

> Your bedded hairs, like life in excrements,[167]
> Start up and stand on end. O gentle son,
135   Upon the heat and flame of thy distemper
> Sprinkle cool patience! Whereon do you look?

HAMLET: On him, on him! Look you how pale he glares!
> His form and cause conjoin'd, preaching to stones,
> Would make them capable.—Do not look upon me,
140   Lest with this piteous action you convert
> My stern effects. Then what I have to do
> Will want true colour—tears perchance for blood.

QUEEN: To whom do you speak this?

HAMLET: Do you see nothing there?

145 QUEEN: Nothing at all; yet all that is I see.

HAMLET: Nor did you nothing hear?

QUEEN: No, nothing but ourselves.

HAMLET: Why, look you there! Look how it steals away!
> My father, in his habit as he liv'd!
150   Look where he goes even now out at the portal!

Exit Ghost.

[168]*invention*

QUEEN: This is the very coinage[168] of your brain.
> This bodiless creation ecstasy
> Is very cunning in.

HAMLET: Ecstasy?

[169]*evenly*

155   My pulse as yours doth temperately[169] keep time
> And makes as healthful music. It is not madness
> That I have utt'red. Bring me to the test,
> And I the matter will reword; which madness

[170]*run away*

> Would gambol[170] from. Mother, for love of grace,

[171]*balm*

160   Lay not that flattering unction[171] to your soul
> That not your trespass but my madness speaks.
> It will but skin and film the ulcerous place,
> Whiles rank corruption, mining all within,
> Infects unseen. Confess yourself to heaven;
165   Repent what's past; avoid what is to come;
> And do not spread the compost on the weeds

To make them ranker. Forgive me this my virtue;
For in the fatness of these pursy[172] times
Virtue itself of vice must pardon beg

172*flabby*

170　Yea, curb[173] and woo for leave to do him good.

173*stoop*

QUEEN: O Hamlet, thou hast cleft my heart in twain.

HAMLET: O, throw away the worser part of it,
And live the purer with the other half,
Good night—but go not to my uncle's bed.

175　Assume a virtue, if you have it not.
That monster, custom, who all sense doth eat
Of habits evil, is angel yet in this,
That to the use of actions fair and good
He likewise gives a frock or livery,

180　That aptly is put on. Refrain to-night,
And that shall lend a kind of easiness
To the next abstinence; the next more easy;
For use almost can change the stamp of nature,
And [either master] the devil, or throw him out[174]

174*Some editors say a word is missing in this line.*

185　With wondrous potency. Once more, good night;
And when you are desirous to be blest,
I'll blessing beg of you. For this same lord,
I do repent; but heaven hath pleas'd it so,
To punish me with this, and this with me,

190　That I must be their scourge and minister.
I will bestow him, and will answer well
The death I gave him. So again, good night.
I must be cruel, only to be kind;
Thus bad begins, and worse remains behind.

195　One word more, good lady.

QUEEN: What shall I do?

HAMLET: Not this, by no means, that I bid you do:
Let the bloat King tempt you again to bed;
Pinch wanton on your cheek; call you his mouse;

200　And let him, for a pair of reechy[175] kisses,
Or paddling in your neck with his damn'd fingers,
Make you to ravel[176] all this matter out,
That I essentially am not in madness,
But mad in craft. 'Twere good you let him know;

175*filthy*

176*untangle*

205　For who that's but a queen, fair, sober, wise,
Would from a paddock,[177] from a bat, a gib[178]

177*toad*

178*tomcat*

Such dear concernings hide? Who would do so?
No, in despite of sense and secrecy,
Unpeg the basket on the house's top,
210   Let the birds fly, and like the famous ape,
To try conclusions, in the basket creep
And break your own neck down.[179]

QUEEN: Be thou assur'd, if words be made of breath,
And breath of life, I have no life to breathe
215   What thou hast said to me.

HAMLET: I must to England; you know that?

QUEEN: Alack,
I had forgot! 'Tis so concluded on.

HAMLET: There's letters seal'd; and my two schoolfellows,
220   Whom I will trust as I will adders[180] fang'd,
They bear the mandate; they must sweep my way
And marshal[181] me to knavery. Let it work;
For 'tis the sport to have the enginer[182]
Hoist[183] with his own petard;[184] and't shall go hard
225   But I will delve[185] one yard below their mines
And blow them at the moon. O, 'tis most sweet
When in one line two crafts directly meet.
This man shall set me packing:
I'll lug the guts into the neighbour room.
230   Mother, good night. Indeed, this counsellor
Is now most still, most secret, and most grave,
Who was in life a foolish prating[186] knave.
Come, sir, to draw toward an end with you.
Good night, mother.

They exit, [Hamlet, tugging in Polonius.]

[handwritten: Going to kill them before they kill him]

179 *The story to which this alludes has been lost.*

180 *poisonous snakes*

181 *lead*

182 *engineer*

183 *blown up*

184 *bomb*

185 *dig*

186 *babbling*

[ACT IV]

[SCENE I]
[Elsinore. A room in the Castle.]

[Enter King and Queen, with Rosencrantz and Guildenstern.]

KING: There's matter in these sighs. These profound heaves
You must translate, 'tis fit we understand them.
Where is your son?
QUEEN: Bestow this place on us a little while.
                              [Rosencrantz and Guildenstern exit.]
5   Ah, mine own lord, what have I seen tonight!
KING: What, Gertrude? How does Hamlet?
QUEEN: Mad as the sea and wind when both contend
Which is the mightier. In his lawless fit,
Behind the arras hearing something stir,
10   Whips out his rapier, cries 'A rat, a rat!'
And in this brainish[1] apprehension kills   ¹*deluded*
The unseen good old man.
KING: O heavy deed!
It had been so with us, had we been there.
15   His liberty is full of threats to all,
To you yourself, to us, to everyone.
Alas, how shall this bloody deed be answer'd?
It will be laid to us, whose providence[2]   ²*supervision*
Should have kept short, restrain'd, and out of haunt[3]   ³*contact with others*
20   This mad young man. But so much was our love
We would not understand what was most fit,
But, like the owner of a foul disease,
To keep it from divulging,[4] let it feed   ⁴*showing itself*
Even on the pith of life. Where is he gone?
25 QUEEN: To draw apart the body he hath kill'd;
O'er whom his very madness, like some ore

87

Among a mineral of metals base,
Shows itself pure. He weeps for what is done.
KING: O Gertrude, come away!
30   The sun no sooner shall the mountains touch
But we will ship him hence; and this vile deed
We must with all our majesty and skill
Both countenance[5] and excuse.[6] Ho, Guildenstern!

Enter Rosencrantz and Guildenstern.
Friends both, go join you with some further aid.
35   Hamlet in madness hath Polonius slain,
And from his mother's closet hath he dragg'd him.
Go seek him out; speak fair, and bring the body
Into the chapel. I pray you haste in this.
                    [Exeunt Rosencrantz and Guildenstern.]
Come, Gertrude, we'll call up our wisest friends
40   And let them know both what we mean to do
And what's untimely done. So haply slander *Adjective*
Whose whisper o'er the world's diameter,
As level as the cannon to his blank,[7]
Transports his poisoned shot, may miss our name
45   And hit the woundless air.—O, come away!
My soul is full of discord and dismay.

Hopes noone trys to bring them down for what Hamlet did.
                                        Exeunt.

[SCENE II]
[Elsinore.]

Enter Hamlet, Rosencrantz, and others.

HAMLET: Safely stow'd.[8]
GENTLEMEN: *[Within.]* Hamlet! Lord Hamlet!
HAMLET: But soft! What noise? Who calls on Hamlet? O, here
they come.

[Enter Rosencrantz and Guildenstern.]

[5]*confront*
[6]*explain*
[7]*target*
[8]*hidden*

5 ROSENCRANTZ: What have you done, my lord, with the dead
    body?

HAMLET: Compounded it with dust, whereto 'tis kin.

ROSENCRANTZ: Tell us where 'tis, that we may take it thence
    And bear it to the chapel.

10 HAMLET: Do not believe it.

ROSENCRANTZ: Believe what?

HAMLET: That I can keep your counsel, and not mine own.
    Besides, to be demanded of a sponge, what replication
    should be made by the son of a king?

15 ROSENCRANTZ: Take you me for a sponge, my lord?

HAMLET: Ay, sir; that soaks up the King's countenance, his
    rewards, his authorities. But such officers do the King best
    service in the end. He keeps them, like an ape, in the corner
    of his jaw; first mouth'd, to be last swallowed. When he
20   needs what you have glean'd, it is but squeezing you and,
    sponge, you shall be dry again.

ROSENCRANTZ: I understand you not, my lord.

HAMLET: I am glad of it. A knavish speech sleeps in a foolish ear.

ROSENCRANTZ: My lord, you must tell us where the body is and
25   go with us to the King.

HAMLET: The body is with the King, but the King is not with
    the body.
    The King is a thing—

GUILDENSTERN: A thing, my lord?

30 HAMLET: Of nothing. Bring me to him. Hide fox, and all after.[9]

                    Exeunt.

[9] *a call from a
children's game
similar to hide-
and-seek*

[SCENE III]
[Elsinore. A room in the Castle.]

Enter King, and two or three.

KING: I have sent to seek him, and to find the body.
    How dangerous is it that this man goes loose!
    Yet must not we put the strong law on him.
    He's loved of the distracted multitude,
5   Who like not in their judgment, but their eyes;

And where 'tis so, the offender's scourge is weigh'd,
But never the offence. To bear all smooth and even,
This sudden sending him away must seem
Deliberate pause.[10] Diseases desperate grown
10 By desperate appliance[11] are relieved,
Or not at all.

10 *consideration*

11 *treatment*

Enter Rosencrantz and all the rest.
How now, what hath befall'n?
ROSENCRANTZ: Where the dead body is bestow'd, my lord,
We cannot get from him.
15 KING: But where is he?
ROSENCRANTZ: Without, my lord; guarded, to know your pleasure.
KING: Bring him before us.
ROSENCRANTZ: Ho, Guildenstern! Bring in my lord.
[Enter Hamlet and Guildenstern with Attendants.]
20 KING: Now, Hamlet, where's Polonius?
HAMLET: At supper.
KING: At supper? Where?
HAMLET: Not where he eats, but where he is eaten. A certain
convocation[12] of politic[13] worms are e'en at him. Your worm
25 is your only emperor for diet. We fat all creatures else to
fat us, and we fat ourselves for maggots. Your fat king and
your lean beggar is but variable service, two dishes, but to
one table. That's the end.
KING: Alas, alas!
30 HAMLET: A man may fish with the worm that hath eat of a
king, and eat of the fish that hath fed of that worm.
KING: What dost thou mean by this?
HAMLET: Nothing but to show you how a king may go a progress through the guts of a beggar.
35 KING: Where is Polonius?
HAMLET: In heaven. Send thither to see. If your messenger
find him not there, seek him i' the other place yourself. But
indeed, if you find him not within this month, you shall
nose him as you go up the stair, into the lobby.
40 KING: Go seek him there.
HAMLET: He will stay till you come.
KING: Hamlet, this deed, for thine especial safety—

12 *gathering*

13 *clever, scheming*

[Handwritten margin note:] telling king the worms will eat him too because the worms don't care he's a king too.

[Handwritten margin note:] telling him If you send someone to heaven to look for him & they don't find him he can look in Hell himself.

[Handwritten note at bottom:] telling him that Polonius is dead & his body is decomposing.

Which we do tender[14] as we dearly grieve

For that which thou hast done—must send thee hence

45   With fiery quickness. Therefore prepare thyself.

The bark[15] is ready and the wind at help,

The associates tend, and everything is bent

For England.

HAMLET: For England?

50   KING: Ay, Hamlet.

HAMLET: Good.

KING: So is it, if thou knew'st our purposes.

HAMLET: I see a cherub that sees them. But come, for England!

Farewell, dear mother.

55   KING: Thy loving father, Hamlet.

HAMLET: My mother! Father and mother is man and wife;

man and wife is one flesh; and so, my mother. Come, for

England!   *Exit.*

KING: Follow him at foot. Tempt him with speed aboard.

60   Delay it not; I'll have him hence tonight.

Away! for every thing is seal'd and done

That else leans on the affair. Pray you, make haste.

And, England, if my love thou hold'st at aught—

As my great power thereof may give thee sense,

65   Since yet thy cicatrice[16] looks raw and red

After the Danish sword, and thy free[17] awe[18]

Pays homage to us—thou mayst not coldly[19] set

Our sovereign process, which imports at full,

By letters congruing[20] to that effect,

70   The present death of Hamlet. Do it, England;

For like the hectic[21] in my blood he rages,

And thou must cure me. Till I know 'tis done,

Howe'er my haps, my joys were ne'er begun.

                                                    Exit.

[margin notes:]

[14]*care about*

[15]*ship*

saying you're one & married to my mom so you're a lady

[16]*scar*

[17]*voluntary*

[18]*respect*

[19]*unenthusiastically*

[20]*agreeing*

[21]*fever*

King Claudius going to get England to kill Hamlet.

Sending Hamlet to deliver letters that say to kill him.

[SCENE IV]
[A plain in Denmark.]

Enter Fortinbras with his Army over the stage.

FORTINBRAS: Go, Captain, from me greet the Danish king.
   Tell him that by his license Fortinbras
   Craves the conveyance²² of a promised march
   Over his kingdom. You know the rendezvous.
5   If that his Majesty would aught with us,
   We shall express our duty in his eye;
   And let him know so.
CAPTAIN: I will do't, my lord.
FORTINBRAS: Go softly on. *[Exit Fortinbras and Forces.]*

Enter Hamlet, Rosencrantz, and others.

10 HAMLET: Good sir, whose powers are these?
CAPTAIN: They are of Norway, sir.
HAMLET: How purposed, sir, I pray you?
CAPTAIN: Against some part of Poland.
HAMLET: Who commands them, sir?
15 CAPTAIN: The nephew to old Norway, Fortinbras.
HAMLET: Goes it against the main of Poland, sir,
   Or for some frontier?
CAPTAIN: Truly to speak, and with no addition,
   We go to gain a little patch of ground
20   That hath in it no profit but the name.
   To pay five ducats, five, I would not farm it;
   Nor will it yield to Norway or the Pole
   A ranker rate, should it be sold in fee.
HAMLET: Why, then the Polack never will defend it.
25 CAPTAIN: Yes, it is already garrison'd.   *Already defended*
HAMLET: Two thousand souls and twenty thousand ducats
   Will not debate the question of this straw.
   This is the imposthume²³ of much wealth and peace,
   That inward breaks, and shows no cause without
30   Why the man dies. I humbly thank you, sir.
CAPTAIN: God be wi' you, sir.
ROSENCRANTZ: Will't please you go, my lord?

²²*escort*

²³*festering sore*

land doesn't matter only going to say they won. Hamlet upset about this land

HAMLET: I'll be with you straight. Go a little before.
How all occasions do inform against me

[handwritten: what good am I if I just eat & Sleep all day]

35   And spur my dull revenge! What is a man,
If his chief good and market of his time
Be but to sleep and feed? A beast, no more.
Sure, he that made us with such large discourse,[24]   [24]*ability to reason*
Looking before and after, gave us not
40   That capability and godlike reason
To fust[25] in us unused. Now, whether it be   [25]*mold*
Bestial oblivion, or some craven[26] scruple   [26]*cowardly*
Of thinking too precisely on the event—
A thought which, quarter'd, hath but one part wisdom
45   And ever three parts coward—I do not know
Why yet I live to say 'This thing's to do,'
Sith I have cause, and will, and strength, and means
To do't. Examples gross as earth exhort me.
Witness this army, of such mass and charge,
50   Led by a delicate and tender prince,
Whose spirit with divine ambition puff'd,
Makes mouths at the invisible event,
Exposing what is mortal and unsure
To all that fortune, death, and danger dare,
55   Even for an eggshell. Rightly to be great
Is not to stir without great argument,
But greatly to find quarrel in a straw
When honour's at the stake. How stand I then,
That have a father kill'd, a mother stain'd,
60   Excitements of my reason and my blood,
And let all sleep, while to my shame I see
The imminent death of twenty thousand men
That for a fantasy and trick of fame
Go to their graves like beds, fight for a plot[27]   [27]*plot of land*
65   Whereon[28] the numbers cannot try[29] the cause,   [28]*on which*
Which is not tomb enough and continent[30]   [29]*fight for*
To hide the slain? O, from this time forth,   [30]*container*
My thoughts be bloody, or be nothing worth!

                                                  Exit.

[handwritten: Can't believe what's going to happen for this land. Upset because 20,000 men are going to die for nothing. Land is to small to bury everyone fighting for.]

[SCENE V]
[Elsinore. A room in the Castle.]

Enter Horatio, Gertrude, and a Gentleman.

QUEEN: I will not speak with her.
GENTLEMAN: She is importunate, indeed distract. Her mood
    will needs be pitied.
QUEEN: What would she have?
5 GENTLEMAN: She speaks much of her father; says she hears
    There's tricks[31] i' the world, and hems,[32] and beats her
        heart;
    Spurns enviously at straws; speaks things in doubt,
    That carry but half sense. Her speech is nothing,
10   Yet the unshaped use of it doth move
    The hearers to collection; they aim at it,
    And botch the words up fit to their own thoughts;
    Which, as her winks and nods and gestures yield them,
    Indeed would make one think there might be thought,
15   Though nothing sure, yet much unhappily.
HORATIO: 'Twere good she were spoken with; for she may
      strew
    Dangerous conjectures in ill-breeding minds.
    Let her come in.   *[Exit Horatio.]*
20 QUEEN: To my sick soul, as sin's true nature is,
    Each toy[33] seems prologue to some great amiss.
    So full of artless[34] jealousy is guilt
    It spills itself in fearing to be spilt.

[Enter Gentleman, with Ophelia distracted.]

OPHELIA: Where is the beauteous Majesty of Denmark?
25 QUEEN: How now, Ophelia?
OPHELIA: *[Sings.]*

        How should I your true love know
          From another one?
        By his cockle hat[35] and staff
30   And his sandal shoon.[36]

---

[31]*deceit*

[32]*clears her throat*

[33]*small thing*

[34]*unintentional*

[35]*hat with a shell*†

[36]*shoes*

QUEEN: Alas, sweet lady, what imports this song?

OPHELIA: Say you? Nay, pray you, mark.

    [*Sings.*]   He is dead and gone, lady,

                   He is dead and gone;

35   At his head a grass-green turf,

                   At his heels a stone.

    O, ho!

QUEEN: Nay, but Ophelia—

OPHELIA: Pray you, mark.

40   [*Sings.*]   White his shroud as the mountain snow—

Enter King.

QUEEN: Alas, look here, my lord!

OPHELIA: [*Sings.*]

                  Larded[37] all with sweet flowers;

                   Which bewept to the grave did not go

45   With true-love showers.

KING: How do you, pretty lady?

OPHELIA: Well, God 'eild[38] you! They say the owl[39] was a baker's daughter.

    Lord, we know what we are, but know not what we may be.

50   God be at your table!

KING: Conceit upon her father.

OPHELIA: Pray let's have no words of this; but when they ask, you what it means, say you this:

    [*Sings.*]

                  Tomorrow is Saint Valentine's day,

55   All in the morning betime,

                  And I a maid at your window,

                   To be your Valentine.

                  Then up he rose and donn'd his clo'es

                   And dupp'd[40] the chamber door,

60   Let in the maid, that out a maid

                   Never departed more.

KING: Pretty Ophelia!

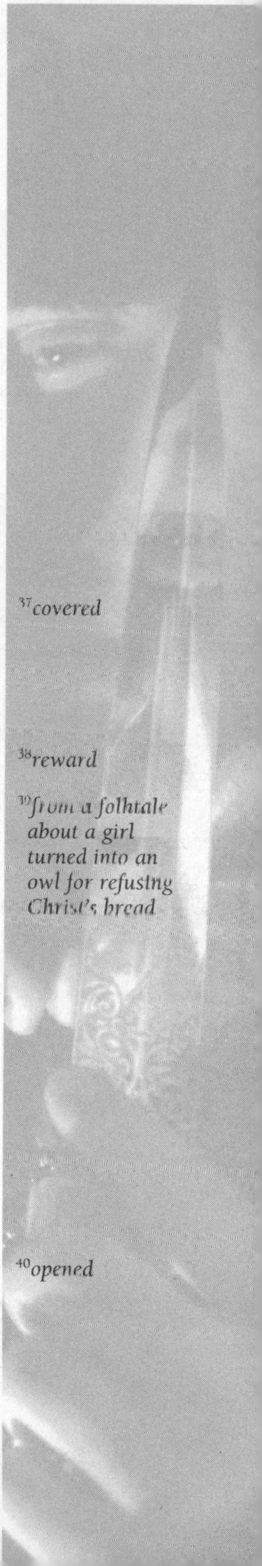

[37] *covered*

[38] *reward*

[39] *from a folktale about a girl turned into an owl for refusing Christ's bread*

[40] *opened*

[Handwritten marginalia: "About having Sex"; "maid - virgin"]

OPHELIA: Indeed, without an oath, I'll make an end on't!
[Sings.]

[41]Jesus

65

By Gis[41] and by Saint Charity,
    Alack, and fie for shame!
Young men will do't if they come to't

[42]God

    By Cock,[42] they are to blame.

Quoth she, 'Before you tumbled me,
    You promis'd me to wed.'

(He answers:)

70

'So would I 'a' done, by yonder sun,
    An thou hadst not come to my bed.'

KING: How long hath she been thus?
OPHELIA: I hope all will be well. We must be patient. But I
cannot choose but weep, to think they would lay him i' the

75   cold ground. My brother shall know of it. And so I thank
you for your good counsel. Come, my coach! Good night,
ladies. Good night, sweet ladies. Good night, good night.
                        [Exit]
KING: Follow her close; give her good watch, I pray you.
    O, this is the poison of deep grief; it springs

80   All from her father's death. O Gertrude, Gertrude,
When sorrows come, they come not single spies.
But in battalions! First, her father slain;
Next, your son gone, and he most violent author

[43]exile

Of his own just remove;[43] the people muddied,[44]

[44]confused

85   Thick and unwholesome in their thoughts and whispers,
For good Polonius' death, and we have done but greenly,

[45]hastily

In hugger-mugger[45] to inter[46] him; poor Ophelia

[46]bury

Divided from herself and her fair judgment,
Without the which we are pictures, or mere beasts;

90   Last, and as much containing as all these,
Her brother is in secret come from France;

[47]whisperers

Feeds on his wonder, keeps himself in clouds,

[48]real subject
  matter

And wants not buzzers[47] to infect his ear
With pestilent speeches of his father's death,

[49]lacking

95   Wherein necessity, of matter[48] beggar'd,[49]
Will nothing stick[50] our person to arraign

[50]hesitate

In ear and ear. O my dear Gertrude, this,

Like to a murdering-piece,[51] in many places
Gives me superfluous death.   *A noise within.*
100 QUEEN: Alack, what noise is this?
KING: Where are my Switzers?[52] Let them guard the door.

Enter another Gentleman.
What is the matter?
GENTLEMAN: Save yourself, my lord.
The ocean, overpeering[53] of his list,[54]
105 Eats not the flats[55] with more impetuous haste
Than young Laertes, in a riotous head,[56]
O'erbears your offices. The rabble call him lord;
And, as[57] the world were now but to begin,
Antiquity forgot, custom not known—
110 The ratifiers and props of every word—
They cry 'Choose we! Laertes shall be king!'
Caps, hands and tongues applaud it to the clouds,
'Laertes shall be king! Laertes king!'   *A noise within.*
QUEEN: How cheerfully on the false trail they cry.
115 O, this is counter,[58] you false Danish dogs!

Enter Laertes with others.

KING: The doors are broke.
LAERTES: Where is this King? Sirs, stand you all without.
ALL: No, let's come in!
LAERTES: I pray you give me leave.
120 ALL: We will, we will!
LAERTES: I thank you. Keep the door.
O thou vile king,
Give me my father!
QUEEN: Calmly, good Laertes.
125 LAERTES: That drop of blood that's calm proclaims me bastard;
Cries cuckold[59] to my father; brands the harlot
Even here, between the chaste unsmirched brows
Of my true mother.
KING: What is the cause, Laertes,
130 That thy rebellion looks so giant-like?
Let him go, Gertrude. Do not fear our person.
There's such divinity doth hedge[60] a king

[51]*a cannon that fired shrapnel-like ammunition*

[52]*Swiss guards*

[53]*looking beyond*

[54]*boundary*

[55]*shores*

[56]*armed force*

[57]*as if*

[58]*wrong*†

[59]*a man cheated on by his wife*

[60]*surround*

That treason can but peep to what it would,
Acts little of his will. Tell me, Laertes,
135   Why thou art thus incensed. Let him go, Gertrude.
Speak, man.
LAERTES: Where is my father?
KING: Dead.
QUEEN: But not by him!
140 KING: Let him demand his fill.
LAERTES: How came he dead? I'll not be juggled with:
To hell, allegiance! Vows, to the blackest devil!
Conscience and grace, to the profoundest pit!
I dare damnation. To this point I stand,
145   That both the worlds, I give to negligence,
Let come what comes; only I'll be revenged
Most throughly for my father.
KING: Who shall stay you?
LAERTES: My will, not all the world!
150   And for my means, I'll husband[61] them so well,
They shall go far with little.
KING: Good Laertes,
If you desire to know the certainty
Of your dear father's death, is't writ in your revenge
155   That, swoopstake,[62] you will draw both friend and foe,
Winner and loser?
LAERTES: None but his enemies.
KING: Will you know them then?
LAERTES: To his good friends thus wide I'll ope my arms
160   And, like the kind life-rendering[63] pelican,
Repast[64] them with my blood. *Gory*
KING: Why, now you speak
Like a good child and a true gentleman.
That I am guiltless of your father's death,
165   And am most sensibly in grief for it,
It shall as level[65] to your judgment pierce
As day does to your eye.   [*A noise within.*]
LAERTES: Let her come in.
How now? What noise is that?

Enter Ophelia.
170   O heat, dry up my brains! Tears seven times salt,
Burn out the sense and virtue of mine eye!

[61]*manage*

[62]*all at once*

[63]*The pelican was thought to feed its young with its own blood.*

[64]*feed*

[65]*plain*

By heaven, thy madness shall be paid with weight,
Till our scale turn the beam. O rose of May!
Dear maid, kind sister, sweet Ophelia!
175   O heavens! is't possible a young maid's wits
Should be as mortal as an old man's life?
Nature is fine[66] in love, and where 'tis fine,

[66]*refined*

It sends some precious instance of itself
After the thing it loves.
180 OPHELIA: *[Sings.]*

> They bore him barefac'd on the bier[67]
> (Hey non nony, nony, hey nony)
> And on his grave rain'd many a tear.

[67]*coffin-stand*

Fare you well, my dove!
185 LAERTES: Hadst thou thy wits, and didst persuade revenge,
It could not move thus.
  OPHELIA: You must sing 'down a-down,' and you 'Call him
a-down-a.' O, how the wheel[68] becomes it! It is the false stew-
ard, that stole his master's daughter.

[68]*chorus*

190 LAERTES: This nothing's more than matter.
  OPHELIA: There's rosemary,[69] that's for remembrance. Pray you,
love, remember. And there is pansies, that's for thoughts.
  LAERTES: A document in madness! Thoughts and remembrance
fitted.

[69]*Ophelia begins
to throw flowers,
each of which has
symbolic meaning:
fennel - flattery
columbine - cuck-
oldry
rue - pity
daisy - false love
violet - faithfulness*

195 OPHELIA: There's fennel for you, and columbines. There's rue for
you, and here's some for me. We may call it herb of grace o'
Sundays. O, you must wear your rue with a difference! There's
a daisy. I would give you some violets, but they wither'd all
when my father died. They say he made a good end—

200   *[Sings.]*   For bonny sweet Robin is all my joy.

  LAERTES: Thought and affliction, passion, hell itself,
She turns to favour and to prettiness.
  OPHELIA: *[Sings.]*

> And will he not come again?
205   And will he not come again?
>   No, no, he is dead;
>   Go to thy deathbed;
> He never will come again.

His beard was as white as snow,

All flaxen[70] was his poll.[71]

210   He is gone, he is gone,

And we cast away moan.

God 'a'mercy on his soul!

And of all Christian souls, I pray God. God be wi' you.

Exit.

LAERTES: Do you see this, O God?

215 KING: Laertes, I must commune with your grief,

Or you deny me right. Go but apart,

Make choice of whom your wisest friends you will,

And they shall hear and judge 'twixt you and me.

If by direct or by collateral[72] hand

220   They find us touch'd,[73] we will our kingdom give,

Our crown, our life, and all that we call ours,

To you in satisfaction;[74] but if not,

Be you content to lend your patience to us,

And we shall jointly labour with your soul

225   To give it due content.

LAERTES: Let this be so.

His means of death, his obscure burial—

No trophy, sword, nor hatchment[75] o'er his bones,

No noble rite nor formal ostentation,[76]

230   Cry to be heard, as 'twere from heaven to earth,

That I must call't in question.

KING: So you shall;

And where the offence is let the great axe fall.

I pray you go with me.

Exeunt.

[SCENE VI]
[Elsinore.]

Enter Horatio and others.

HORATIO: What are they that would speak with me?
SERVANT: Seafaring men, sir. They say they have letters for you.
HORATIO: Let them come in.   *[Exit Servant.]*
    I do not know from what part of the world
5   I should be greeted, if not from Lord Hamlet.

Enter Sailors.

SAILOR: God bless you, sir.
HORATIO: Let him bless thee too.
SAILOR: He shall, sir, an't please him. There's a letter for you, sir.
    It comes from the ambassador that was bound for England—
10   if your name be Horatio, as I am let to know it is.
HORATIO: *[Reads the letter]* 'Horatio, when thou shalt have overlook'd
    this, give these fellows some means to the King. They have letters
    for him. Ere we were two days old at sea, a pirate of very warlike
    appointment[77] gave us chase. Finding ourselves too slow of sail, we
15   put on a compelled valour, and in the grapple[78] I boarded them. On
    the instant they got clear of our ship; so I alone became their prisoner.
    They have dealt with me like thieves of mercy; but they knew what
    they did: I am to do a good turn for them. Let the King have the letters
    I have sent, and repair thou to me with as much speed as thou wouldst
20   fly death. I have words to speak in thine ear will make thee dumb; yet
    are they much too light for the bore of the matter. These good fellows
    will bring thee where I am. Rosencrantz and Guildenstern hold their
    course for England. Of them I have much to tell thee. Farewell.
          He that thou knowest thine, Hamlet '

25   Come, I will give you way for these your letters,
    And do't the speedier that you may direct me
    To him from whom you brought them.

                    Exeunt.

[77] *equipment*
[78] *struggle*

[SCENE VII]
[Elsinore.]

Enter King and Laertes.

⁷⁹*innocence*

KING: Now must your conscience my acquittance[79] seal,
       And you must put me in your heart for friend,
       Sith you have heard, and with a knowing ear,
       That he which hath your noble father slain
5   Pursued my life.
LAERTES: It well appears. But tell me
       Why you proceeded not against these feats
       So crimeful and so capital in nature,
       As by your safety, wisdom, all things else,
10   You mainly were stirr'd up.
KING: O, for two special reasons,

⁸⁰*lacking strength*

       Which may to you, perhaps, seem much unsinew'd,[80]
       But yet to me they're strong. The Queen his mother
       Lives almost by his looks; and for myself—
15   My virtue or my plague, be it either which—

⁸¹*united, connected*
⁸²*orbit*

       She's so conjunctive[81] to my life and soul
       That, as the star moves not but in his sphere,[82]
       I could not but by her. The other motive

⁸³*trial*
⁸⁴*people*

       Why to a public count[83] I might not go
20   Is the great love the general gender[84] bear him,
       Who, dipping all his faults in their affection,
       Would, like the spring that turneth wood to stone,

⁸⁵*shackles*
⁸⁶*constructed*
⁸⁷*bounced back*

       Convert his gyves[85] to graces; so that my arrows,
       Too slightly timber'd[86] for so loud a wind,
25   Would have reverted[87] to my bow again,
       And not where I had aim'd them.
LAERTES: And so have I a noble father lost;
       A sister driven into desperate terms,
       Whose worth, if praises may go back again,
30   Stood challenger on mount of all the age
       For her perfections. But my revenge will come.
KING: Break not your sleeps for that. You must not think
       That we are made of stuff so flat and dull
       That we can let our beard be shook with danger,

⁸⁸*entertainment*

35   And think it pastime.[88] You shortly shall hear more.

I loved your father, and we love ourself,
And that, I hope, will teach you to imagine—

Enter a Messenger with letters.
How now? What news?
MESSENGER: Letters, my lord, from Hamlet.
40   This to your Majesty; this to the Queen.
KING: From Hamlet? Who brought them?
MESSENGER: Sailors, my lord, they say; I saw them not.
They were given me by Claudio; he receiv'd them
Of him that brought them.
45 KING: Laertes, you shall hear them.
Leave us.   *[Exit Messenger.]*

[Reads] High and mighty, you shall know I am set naked[89] on your   [89]*with no possessions*
kingdom. Tomorrow shall I beg leave to see your kingly eyes, when I
shall, first asking your pardon, thereunto recount the occasion of my
50   sudden and more strange return.

                                          HAMLET.

What should this mean? Are all the rest come back?
Or is it some abuse, and no such thing?
LAERTES: Know you the hand?
KING: 'Tis Hamlet's character. 'Naked'—
55   And in a postscript here, he says 'Alone.'
Can you advise me?
LAERTES: I'm lost in it, my lord. But let him come.
It warms the very sickness in my heart
That I shall live and tell him to his teeth,
60   'Thus diddest thou.'
KING: If it be so, Laertes
As how should it be so? how otherwise?—
Will you be ruled by me?
LAERTES: Ay my lord,
65   So you will not o'errule me to a peace.
KING: To thine own peace. If he be now return'd
As checking[90] at his voyage, and that he means   [90]*turning away from*
No more to undertake it, I will work him
To an exploit, now ripe in my device,[91]   [91]*scheme*
70   Under the which he shall not choose but fall;
And for his death no wind of blame shall breathe,

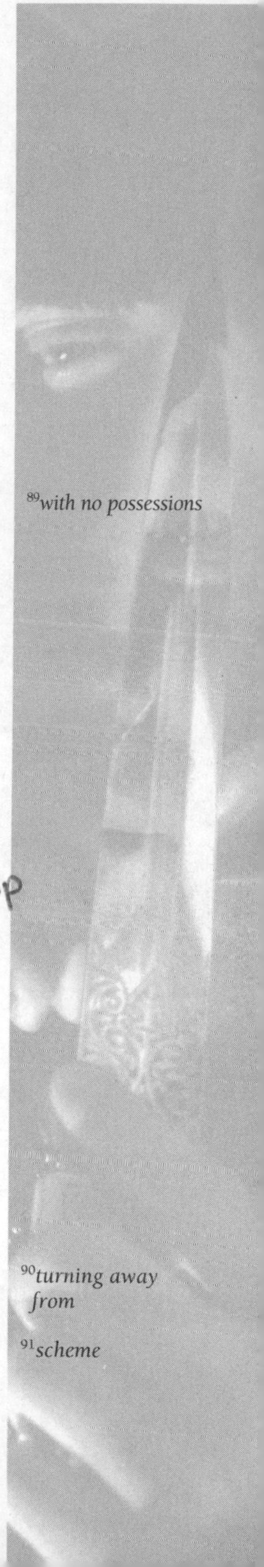

(handwritten note: Hamlet's alone & needs help)

92*excuse*

But even his mother shall uncharge[92] the practice,
And call it accident.

LAERTES: My lord, I will be ruled;

75   The rather, if you could devise it so

93*instrument [of his death]*

That I might be the organ.[93]

KING: It falls right.
You have been talk'd of since your travel much,
And that in Hamlet's hearing, for a quality

80   Wherein they say you shine. Your sum of parts
Did not together pluck such envy from him
As did that one; and that, in my regard,

94*most unimportant*

95*position*

Of the unworthiest[94] siege.[95]

LAERTES: What part is that, my lord?

85 KING: A very ribbon in the cap of youth,
Yet needful too; for youth no less becomes

96*garments*

The light and careless livery that it wears
Than settled age his sables and his weeds,[96]

97*prosperity*

98*seriousness*

Importing health[97] and graveness.[98] Two months since

90   Here was a gentleman of Normandy—
I have seen myself, and served against, the French,
And they can well on horseback; but this gallant
Had witchcraft in't. He grew unto his seat,
And to such wondrous doing brought his horse

99*made part of the body*

95   As had he been incorpsed[99] and demi-natured[100]

100*given character-istics of*

With the brave beast. So far he topp'd[101] my thought[102]
That I, in forgery of shapes and tricks,

101*exceeded*

Come short of what he did.

LAERTES: A Norman was't?

102*imagination*

100 KING: A Norman.

LAERTES: Upon my life, Lamord.

KING: The very same.

LAERTES: I know him well. He is the brooch indeed
And gem of all the nation.

105 KING: He made confession of you;
And gave you such a masterly report,
For art and exercise in your defence,
And for your rapier most especial,
That he cried out 'twould be a sight indeed

103*swordsmen*

110   If one could match you. The scrimers[103] of their nation
He swore had neither motion, guard, nor eye,
If you opposed them. Sir, this report of his

Did Hamlet so envenom with his envy
That he could nothing do but wish and beg
115 Your sudden coming o'er to play with him.
Now, out of this—
  LAERTES: What out of this, my lord?
  KING: Laertes, was your father dear to you?
Or are you like the painting of a sorrow,
120 A face without a heart,
  LAERTES: Why ask you this?
  KING: Not that I think you did not love your father,
But that I know love is begun by time,
And that I see, in passages[104] of proof,[105]   [104]*cases*
125 Time qualifies[106] the spark and fire of it.   [105]*experience*
There lives within the very flame of love   [106]*weakens*
A kind of wick or snuff that will abate it;
And nothing is at a like goodness still;
For goodness, growing to a pleurisy,[107]   [107]*a disease*
130 Dies in his own too much. That we would do,
We should do when we would; for this 'would' changes,
And hath abatements and delays as many
As there are tongues, are hands, are accidents;
And then this 'should' is like a spendthrift[108] sigh,   [108]*wasteful*
135 That hurts[109] by easing. But to the quick o' the ulcer!   [109]*A sigh was*
Hamlet comes back. What would you undertake   *thought to cause*
To show yourself your father's son in deed   *injury by drawing*
More than in words?   *blood from the*
  LAERTES: To cut his throat i' the church.   *heart.*
140 KING: No place indeed should murder sanctuarize;[110]   [110]*protect from*
Revenge should have no bounds. But, good Laertes,   *punishment*
Will you do this? Keep close within your chamber.
Hamlet return'd shall know you are come home.
We'll put on those shall praise your excellence
145 And set a double varnish on the fame
The Frenchman gave you, bring you in fine[111] together   [111]*finally*
And wager on your heads. He, being remiss,[112]   [112]*negligent*
Most generous and free from all contriving,
Will not peruse the foils; so that with ease,
150 Or with a little shuffling, you may choose
A sword unbated,[113] and in a pass of practice,   [113]*not tipped*
Requite him for your father.
  LAERTES: I will do't!

¹¹⁴*ointment*

¹¹⁵*an unqualified
    doctor*

¹¹⁶*medical plaster*

¹¹⁷*herbs*

¹¹⁸*show*

¹¹⁹*blow up*

¹²⁰*abilities*

¹²¹*decorated cup*

¹²²*purpose*

¹²³*grey*

¹²⁴*freely-speaking*

¹²⁵*chaste*

¹²⁶*hanging*

¹²⁷*crowning*

¹²⁸*hateful*

And for that purpose I'll anoint my sword.
155   I bought an unction[114] of a mountebank,[115]
So mortal that but dip a knife in it,
Where it draws blood no cataplasm[116] so rare,
Collected from all simples[117] that have virtue
Under the moon, can save the thing from death
160   This is but scratch'd withal. I'll touch my point
With this contagion, that, if I gall him slightly,
It may be death.

KING: Let's further think of this,
Weigh what convenience both of time and means
165   May fit us to our shape. If this should fail,
And that our drift look[118] through our bad performance.
'Twere better not assay'd. Therefore this project
Should have a back or second, that might hold
If this did blast[119] in proof. Soft! let me see.
170   We'll make a solemn wager on your cunnings—[120]
I ha't!
When in your motion you are hot and dry—
As make your bouts more violent to that end—
And that he calls for drink, I'll have prepared him
175   A chalice[121] for the nonce;[122] whereon but sipping,
If he by chance escape your venom'd stuck,
Our purpose may hold there. But stay, what noise?

Enter Queen.
How now, sweet Queen?

QUEEN: One woe doth tread upon another's heel,
180   So fast they follow. Your sister's drown'd, Laertes.

LAERTES: Drown'd! O, where?

QUEEN: There is a willow grows askant a brook,
That shows his hoary[123] leaves in the glassy stream.
Therewith fantastic garlands did she make
185   Of crow-flowers, nettles, daisies, and long purples,
That liberal[124] shepherds give a grosser name,
But our cold[125] maids do dead men's fingers call them.
There on the pendant[126] boughs her coronet[127] weeds
Clambering to hang, an envious[128] sliver broke,
190   When down her weedy trophies and herself
Fell in the weeping brook. Her clothes spread wide

And, mermaid-like, awhile they bore her up;
Which time she chanted snatches of old lauds,[129]
As one incapable[130] of her own distress,
195   Or like a creature native and indued[131]
Unto that element; but long it could not be
Till that her garments, heavy with their drink,
Pull'd the poor wretch from her melodious lay[132]
To muddy death.
200 LAERTES: Alas, then she is drown'd?
QUEEN: Drown'd, drown'd.
LAERTES: Too much of water hast thou, poor Ophelia,
And therefore I forbid my tears; but yet
It is our trick;[133] nature her custom holds,
205   Let shame say what it will. When these are gone,
The woman[134] will be out.[135] Adieu, my lord.
I have a speech of fire, that fain would blaze
But that this folly drowns it.   *Exit.*
KING: Let's follow, Gertrude.
210   How much I had to do to calm his rage.
Now fear I this will give it start again;
Therefore let's follow.

                    Exeunt.

[129]*hymns*

[130]*unaware*

[131]*endowed*

[132]*song*

[133]*way*

[134]*womanly side*

[135]*gone*

[ACT V]

[SCENE I]
[Elsinore. A churchyard.]

Enter two Clowns.

FIRST CLOWN: Is she to be buried in Christian burial that wilfully
seeks her own salvation?

SECOND CLOWN: I tell thee she is; therefore make her grave
straight. The crowner[1] hath sat on her, and finds it Christian
5   burial.

FIRST CLOWN: How can that be, unless she drown'd herself in
her own defence?

SECOND CLOWN: Why, 'tis found so.

FIRST CLOWN: It must be *se offendendo*;[2] it cannot be else. For
10   here lies the point: if I drown myself wittingly,[3] it argues an
act; and an act hath three branches: it is to act, to do, and to
perform; argal,[4] she drown'd herself wittingly.

SECOND CLOWN: Nay, but hear you, goodman delver—[5]

FIRST CLOWN: Give me leave. Here lies the water—good. Here
15   stands the man—good. If the man go to this water and
drown himself, it is, will he, nill he, he goes. Mark you that.
But if the water come to him and drown him, he drowns not
himself. Argal, he that is not guilty of his own death shortens
not his own life.

20 SECOND CLOWN: But is this law?

FIRST CLOWN: Ay, marry, is't; crowner's quest[6] law.

SECOND CLOWN: Will you ha' the truth on't? If this had not been
a gentlewoman, she should have been buried out o' Christian
burial.

25 FIRST CLOWN: Why, there thou say'st! And the more pity that
great folk should have countenance in this world to drown
or hang themselves more than their even Christian. Come,

---

[1]*coroner*

[2]*the clown's version of "se defenden-do," meaning "in self-defense"*

[3]*intentionally*

[4]*mistake for "ergo," meaning "therefore"*

[5]*digger*

[6]*investigation*

7both "had arms
(limbs)" and "had
a coat of arms"

my spade! There is no ancient gentlemen but gardeners, ditchers, and grave-makers. They hold up Adam's profes-
30   sion.

SECOND CLOWN: Was he a gentleman?

FIRST CLOWN: A was the first that ever bore arms.[7]

SECOND CLOWN: Why, he had none.

FIRST CLOWN: What, art a heathen? How dost thou under-
35   stand the Scripture? The Scripture says Adam digged. Could he dig without arms? I'll put another question to thee. If thou answerest me not to the purpose, confess thyself—

SECOND CLOWN: Go to!

40 FIRST CLOWN: What is he that builds stronger than either the mason, the shipwright, or the carpenter?

SECOND CLOWN: The gallows-maker; for that frame outlives a thousand tenants.

FIRST CLOWN: I like thy wit well, in good faith. The gallows
45   does well. But how does it well? It does well to those that do ill. Now, thou dost ill to say the gallows is built stronger than the church. Argal, the gallows may do well to thee. To't again, come!

SECOND CLOWN: Who builds stronger than a mason, a ship-
50   wright, or a carpenter?

FIRST CLOWN: Ay, tell me that, and unyoke.

SECOND CLOWN: Marry, now I can tell!

FIRST CLOWN: To't.

SECOND CLOWN: Mass, I cannot tell.

8beat

55 FIRST CLOWN: Cudgel[8] thy brains no more about it, for your dull ass will not mend his pace with beating; and when you are asked this question next, say 'A grave-maker.' The houses that he makes last till doomsday. Go, get thee to Yaughan; fetch me a stoup of liquor.

                    [Exit Second Clown.First Clown digs and sings.]

60   In youth when I did love, did love,
                    Methought it was very sweet;
                To contract—O—the time for—a—my behove,
                    O, methought there—a—was nothing—a meet.

Enter Hamlet and Horatio.

HAMLET: Has this fellow no feeling of his business, that he sings
65   at grave-making?

HORATIO: Custom hath made it in him a property of easiness.

HAMLET: 'Tis e'en so. The hand of little employment hath the
daintier sense.

FIRST CLOWN: *[Sings.]*
70
          But age with his stealing steps
            Hath clawed me in his clutch,
          And hath shipped me intil[9] the land,
            As if I had never been such.

                    [Throws up a skull.]

HAMLET: That skull had a tongue in it, and could sing once.
75   How the knave jowls[10] it to the ground, as if 'were Cain's
jawbone, that did the first murder! This might be the pate of
a politician, which this ass now o'erreaches; one that would
circumvent[11] God, might it not?

HORATIO: It might, my lord.

80 HAMLET: Or of a courtier, which could say 'Good morrow, sweet
lord!
How dost thou, sweet lord?' This might be my Lord Such-a-
one, that praised my Lord Such-a one's horse when he went
to beg it, might it not?

85 HORATIO: Ay, my lord.

HAMLET: Why, e'en so! and now my Lady Worm's, chapless,[12]
and knock'd about the mazard[13] with a sexton's spade. Here's
fine revolution, and we had the trick to see't. Did these bones
cost no more the breeding, but to play at loggats[14] with 'em?
90   Mine ache to think on't.

FIRST CLOWN: *[Sings.]*   *Saying they aren't
respecting his skull*

          A pickaxe and a spade, a spade,
           For and a shrouding sheet;
         O, a Pit of clay for to be made
95
           For such a guest is meet.

              [Throws up another skull.]

HAMLET: There's another. Why may not that be the skull of
a lawyer? Where be his quiddities[15] now, his quillets,[16] his
cases, his tenures,[17] and his tricks? Why does he suffer this
rude knave now to knock him about the sconce[18] with a
100 dirty shovel, and will not tell him of his action[19] of battery?[20]
Hum! This fellow might be in's time a great buyer of land,

---

[9]*into*

[10]*throws*

[11]*bypass*

[12]*jawless*
[13]*head*

[14]*a game in which sticks are thrown at a target*

[15]*subtle points*
[16]*petty distinctions*
[17]*titles to real estate*
[18]*head*
[19]*charge*
[20]*personal assault*

²¹*bonds acknowl-
edging a debt*

²²*guarantees of
property*

²³*legal transfers of
property*

²⁴*"end," but Hamlet
also puns on "fine"
meaning "fee,"
"splendid," and
"small-grained"*

²⁵*joint agreements*

²⁶*documents stating
transfer of property*

with his statutes, his recognizances,²¹ his fines, his double
vouchers,²² his recoveries.²³ Is this the fine²⁴ of his fines,
and the recovery of his recoveries, to have his fine pate
105 full of fine dirt? Will his vouchers vouch him no more of
his purchases, and double ones too, than the length and
breadth of a pair of indentures?²⁵ The very conveyances²⁶ of
his lands will hardly lie in this box; and must the inheritor
himself have no more, ha?

110 HORATIO: Not a jot more, my lord.

HAMLET: Is not parchment made of sheepskins?

HORATIO: Ay, my lord, And of calveskins too.

HAMLET: They are sheep and calves which seek out assurance
in that. I will speak to this fellow. Whose grave's this, sir-
115   rah?

FIRST CLOWN: Mine, sir.

> [*Sings.*]
>
> O, a pit of clay for to be made
> For such a guest is meet.

HAMLET: I think it be thine indeed, for thou liest in't.

²⁷*of it*

120 FIRST CLOWN: You lie out on't,²⁷ sir, and therefore 'tis not
yours. For my part, I do not lie in't, yet it is mine.

HAMLET: Thou dost lie in't, to be in't and say it is thine. 'Tis for
the dead, not for the quick; therefore thou liest.

FIRST CLOWN: 'Tis a quick lie, sir; 'twill away again from me
125   to you.

HAMLET: What man dost thou dig it for?

FIRST CLOWN: For no man, sir.

HAMLET: What woman then?

FIRST CLOWN: For none, neither.

130 HAMLET: Who is to be buried in't?

FIRST CLOWN: One that was a woman, sir; but, rest her soul,
she's dead.

HAMLET: How absolute²⁸ the knave is! We must speak by the
card,²⁹ or equivocation³⁰ will undo us. By the Lord, Horatio,
135   this three years I have taken note of it, the age is grown so
picked³¹ that the toe of the peasant comes so near the heel
of the courtier he galls³² his kibe.³³ How long hast thou
been a grave-maker?

²⁸*literal*

²⁹*most accurate
model*†

³⁰*double-meaning*

³¹*refined*

³²*rubs against*

³³*sore on the heel*

FIRST CLOWN: Of all the days i' the year, I came to't that day
140   that our last king Hamlet overcame Fortinbras.

HAMLET: How long is that since?

FIRST CLOWN: Cannot you tell that? Every fool can tell that. It was the very day that young Hamlet was born—he that is mad, and sent into England.

145 HAMLET: Ay, marry, why was he sent into England?

FIRST CLOWN: Why, because a was mad. A shall recover his wits there; or, if a do not, 'tis no great matter there.

HAMLET: Why?

FIRST CLOWN: 'Twill not be seen in him there. There the men
150   are as mad as he.

HAMLET: How came he mad?

FIRST CLOWN: Very strangely, they say.

HAMLET: How 'strangely'?

FIRST CLOWN: Faith, e'en with losing his wits.

155 HAMLET: Upon what ground?

FIRST CLOWN: Why, here in Denmark. I have been sexton here, man and boy, thirty years.

HAMLET: How long will a man lie i' the earth ere he rot?

FIRST CLOWN: I' faith, if he be not rotten before he die—as we
160   have many pocky[34] corses nowadays that will scarce hold the laying in—he will last you some eight year or nine year. A tanner[35] will last you nine year.

HAMLET: Why he more than another?

FIRST CLOWN: Why, sir, his hide is so tanned with his trade that
165   a will keep out water a great while; and your water is a sore decayer of your whoreson dead body. Here's a skull, now. This skull hath lain in the earth three and twenty years.

HAMLET: Whose was it?

FIRST CLOWN: A whoreson, mad fellow's it was. Whose do you
170   think it was?

HAMLET: Nay, I know not.

FIRST CLOWN: A pestilence on him for a mad rogue! A poured a flagon[36] of Rhenish on my head once. This same skull, sir, was Yorick's skull, the King's jester.

175 HAMLET: This?

FIRST CLOWN: E'en that.

HAMLET: *[Takes the skull.]* Alas, poor Yorick! I knew him, Horatio: a fellow of infinite jest, of most excellent fancy. He hath borne me on his back a thousand times. And now how
180   abhorred in my imagination it is! My gorge[37] rises at it. Here

[34] *rotten; marked by smallpox*

[35] *one who tans animal hides*

[36] *pitcher*

[37] *the contents of the stomach*

hung those lips that I have kissed I know not how oft. Where be your gibes[38] now? your gambols?[39] your songs? your flashes of merriment, that were wont to set the table on a roar? Not one now to mock your own grinning? Quite chop-fallen?[40] Now get you to my lady's chamber, and tell her, let her paint an inch thick, to this favour she must come. Make her laugh at that. Prithee, Horatio, tell me one thing.

HORATIO: What's that, my lord?

HAMLET: Dost thou think Alexander[41] looked o' this fashion i' the earth?

HORATIO: E'en so.

HAMLET: And smelt so? Pah!

HORATIO: E'en so, my lord.

HAMLET: To what base uses we may return, Horatio! Why may not imagination trace the noble dust of Alexander till he find it stopping a bung-hole?[42]

HORATIO: 'Twere to consider too curiously, to consider so.

HAMLET: No, faith, not a jot; but to follow him thither with modesty enough, and likelihood to lead it; as thus: Alexander died, Alexander was buried, Alexander returneth into dust; the dust is earth; of earth we make loam;[43] and why of that loam, whereto he was converted, might they not stop a beer barrel?

Imperious Caesar, dead and turn'd to clay,
Might stop a hole to keep the wind away.
O, that that earth, which kept the world in awe
Should patch a wall to expel the winter's flaw!
But soft! but soft awhile! Here comes the King,
The Queen, the courtiers.

[Enter Priests, in procession, corpse of Ophelia, Laertes and Mourners following King, Queen, and Attendants.]

Who is this they follow?
And with such maimed[44] rites? This doth betoken[45]
The corse they follow did with desperate hand
Fordo it own life. 'Twas of some estate.[46]
Couch[47] we awhile, and mark.

LAERTES: What ceremony else?

HAMLET: That is Laertes, a very noble youth. Mark.

LAERTES: What ceremony else?

PRIEST: Her obsequies[48] have been as far enlarged[49]

220   As we have warranty.[50] Her death was doubtful;
And, but that great command o'ersways the order,
She should in ground unsanctified[51] have lodged
Till the last trumpet.[52] For charitable prayers,
Shards, flints, and pebbles should be thrown on her.

225   Yet here she is allow'd her virgin crants,[53]
Her maiden strewments[54] and the bringing home
Of bell and burial.

LAERTES: Must there no more be done?

PRIEST: No more be done.

230   We should profane the service of the dead
To sing a requiem[55] and such rest to her
As to peace-parted souls.

LAERTES: Lay her i' the earth;
And from her fair and unpolluted flesh

235   May violets spring! I tell thee, churlish[56] priest,
A ministering angel shall my sister be
When thou liest howling.

HAMLET: What, the fair Ophelia!

QUEEN: Sweets to the sweet! Farewell.

240   I hoped thou shouldst have been my Hamlet's wife;
I thought thy bride-bed to have deck'd, sweet maid,
And not have strew'd thy grave.

LAERTES: O, treble[57] woe
Fall ten times treble on that cursed head

245   Whose wicked deed thy most ingenious[58] sense
Deprived thee of! Hold off the earth awhile,
Till I have caught her once more in mine arms.

                     [Leaps in the grave.]

Now pile your dust upon the quick and dead
Till of this flat a mountain you have made

250   To o'ertop old Pelion[59] or the skyish head
Of blue Olympus.[60]

HAMLET: What is he whose grief
Bears such an emphasis, whose phrase of sorrow
Conjures the wandering stars and makes them stand

255   Like wonder-wounded hearers? This is I,
Hamlet the Dane.   *[Leaps in after Laertes.]*

[48] *funeral rites*
[49] *extended*
[50] *ability*
[51] *unblessed*
[52] *Judgment Day*
[53] *wreaths*
[54] *grave-flowers*
[55] *funeral chant*
[56] *ungracious*
[57] *triple*
[58] *intelligent*
[59] *a high mountain in Greece*
[60] *the mountain in Greece on which the gods lived*

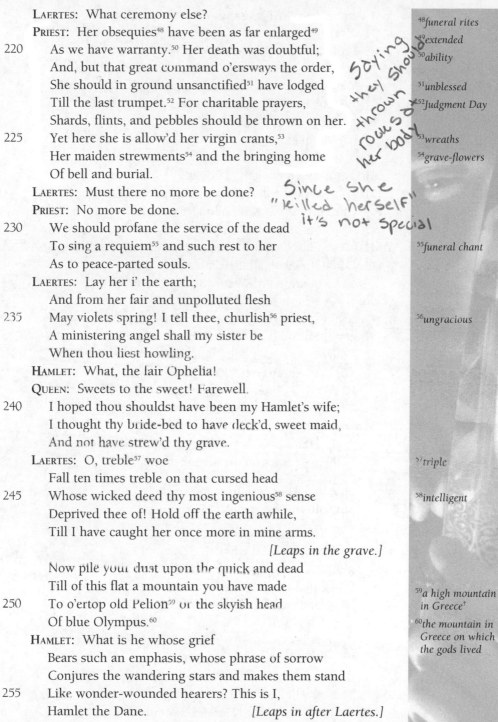

LAERTES: The devil take thy soul!

HAMLET: Thou pray'st not well.
    I prithee, take thy fingers from my throat;

⁶¹*ill-tempered*   260   For, though I am not splenitive⁶¹ and rash,
    Yet have I in me something dangerous,
    Which let thy wisdom fear. Hold off thy hand!

⁶²*apart*   KING: Pluck them asunder.⁶²

QUEEN: Hamlet, Hamlet!

265   ALL: Gentlemen!

HORATIO: Good my lord, be quiet.

⁶³*subject*   HAMLET: Why, I will fight with him upon this theme⁶³
    Until my eyelids will no longer wag.

QUEEN: O my son, what theme?

270   HAMLET: I loved Ophelia. Forty thousand brothers
    Could not, with all their quantity of love,
    Make up my sum. What wilt thou do for her?

KING: O, he is mad, Laertes.

⁶⁴*don't touch*   QUEEN: For love of God, forbear⁶⁴ him!

275   HAMLET: 'Swounds, show me what thou'lt do.
    Woo't weep, woo't fight, woo't fast, woo't tear thyself?

⁶⁵*vinegar*   Woo't drink up eisel,⁶⁵ eat a crocodile?
    I'll do't. Dost thou come here to whine,
    To outface me with leaping in her grave?

280   Be buried quick with her, and so will I.
    And, if thou prate of mountains, let them throw
    Millions of acres on us, till our ground,
    Singeing his pate against the burning zone,

⁶⁶*a mountain in*   Make Ossa⁶⁶ like a wart! Nay, an thou'lt mouth,⁶⁷
Greece

⁶⁷*babble*   285   I'll rant as well as thou.

QUEEN: This is mere madness;
    And thus awhile the fit will work on him.
    Anon, as patient as the female dove

⁶⁸*chicks*   When that her golden couplets⁶⁸ are disclosed,

290   His silence will sit drooping.

HAMLET: Hear you, sir!
    What is the reason that you use me thus?
    I loved you ever. But it is no matter.
    Let Hercules himself do what he may,

295   The cat will mew, and dog will have his day.   *[Exit.]*

KING: I pray thee, good Horatio, wait upon him.

                                                        [Exit Horatio.]

Strengthen your patience in our last night's speech.
We'll put the matter to the present push.—
Good Gertrude, set some watch over your son.
300　This grave shall have a living monument.
An hour of quiet shortly shall we see;
Till then, in patience our proceeding be.

Exeunt.

[SCENE II]
[Elsinore. A hall in the Castle.]

Enter Hamlet and Horatio.

HAMLET: So much for this, sir; now shall you see the other.
　　You do remember all the circumstance?
HORATIO: Remember it, my lord!
HAMLET: Sir, in my heart there was a kind of fighting
5　　That would not let me sleep. Methought I lay
　　Worse than the mutines[69] in the bilboes.[70] Rashly—
　　And praised be rashness, for it let us know,
　　Our indiscretion sometime serves us well
　　When our deep plots do pall;[71] and that should learn us
10　There's a divinity that shapes our ends,
　　Rough-hew them how we will—
HORATIO: That is most certain.
HAMLET: Up from my cabin,
　　My sea-gown scarf'd about me, in the dark
15　Groped I to find out them; had my desire,
　　Fingered their packet, and in fine withdrew
　　To mine own room again, making so bold
　　My fears forgetting manners, to unseal
　　Their grand commission;[72] where I found, Horatio—
20　O royal knavery!—an exact command,
　　Larded with many several sorts of reasons,
　　Importing Denmark's health, and England's too,
　　With, ho! such bugs and goblins in my life,
　　That on the supervise,[73] no leisure[74] bated,[75]

[69]*mutineers; rebels*

[70]*shackles*

[71]*fail*

[72]*task*

[73]*reading of the note*

[74]*delay*

[75]*allowed*

25   No, not to stay the grinding of the axe,
        My head should be struck off.
    HORATIO: Is't possible?
    HAMLET: Here's the commission; read it at more leisure.
        But wilt thou hear me how I did proceed?
30 HORATIO: I beseech you.
    HAMLET: Being thus benetted round with villainies—
        Or[76] I could make a prologue to my brains,
        They had begun the play—I sat me down,
        Devised a new commission, wrote it fair.
35   I once did hold it, as our statists[77] do,
        A baseness[78] to write fair,[79] and labour'd much
        How to forget that learning; but, sir, now
        It did me yeoman's[80] service. Wilt thou know
        The effect of what I wrote?
40 HORATIO: Ay, good my lord.
    HAMLET: An earnest conjuration[81] from the King,
        As England was his faithful tributary,[82]
        As love between them like the palm might flourish,
        As peace should still her wheaten garland[83] wear
45   And stand a comma 'tween their amities,[84]
        And many such like as's of great charge,[85]
        That on the view and knowing of these contents,
        Without debatement further, more or less,
        He should the bearers put to sudden death,
50   Not shriving-time[86] allow'd.
    HORATIO: How was this seal'd?
    HAMLET: Why, even in that was heaven ordinant.[87]
        I had my father's signet[88] in my purse,
        Which was the model of that Danish seal;
55   Folded the writ up in the form of the other,
        Subscribed[89] it, gave't the impression,[90] placed it safely,
        The changeling[91] never known. Now, the next day
        Was our sea-fight; and what to this was sequent[92]
        Thou know'st already.
60 HORATIO: So Guildenstern and Rosencrantz go to't.
    HAMLET: Why, man, they did make love to this employment!
        They are not near my conscience; their defeat
        Does by their own insinuation grow.
        'Tis dangerous when the baser nature comes

[76]*before*

[77]*statesmen*
[78]*lowly skill*
[79]*neatly*
[80]*faithful*†

[81]*request*
[82]*servant nation*
[83]*a wreath symbolic of peace*
[84]*friendships*
[85]*significance*

[86]*confession of sins*

[87]*in control*
[88]*ring with the official seal*

[89]*signed*
[90]*seal*
[91]*substitution*†
[92]*the result*

65   Between the pass[93] and fell[94] incensed points
        Of mighty opposites.
      HORATIO: Why, what a king is this!
      HAMLET: Does it not, think thee, stand me now upon—
        He that hath kill'd my king, and whored my mother;
70   Popp'd in between the election[95] and my hopes;[†]
        Thrown out his angle[96] for my proper[97] life,
        And with such cozenage—is't not perfect conscience
        To quit[98] him with this arm? And is't not to be damn'd
        To let this canker of our nature come
75   In further evil?
      HORATIO: It must be shortly known to him from England
        What is the issue of the business there.
      HAMLET: It will be short; the interim is mine,
        And a man's life's is no more than to say 'One.'
80   But I am very sorry, good Horatio,
        That to Laertes I forgot myself,
        For by the image of my cause I see
        The portraiture of his. I'll court his favours.
        But, sure, the bravery of his grief did put me
85   Into a towering passion.
      HORATIO: Peace, who comes here?

      Enter [young Osric], a courtier.

      OSRIC: Your lordship is right welcome back to Denmark.
      HAMLET: I humbly thank you, sir. *[Aside to Horatio.]* Dost know
        this water-fly?[99]
90   HORATIO: *[Aside to Hamlet.]* No, my good lord.
      HAMLET: *[Aside to Horatio.]* Thy state is the more gracious; for
        'tis a vice to know him. He hath much land, and fertile. Let a
        beast be lord of beasts, and his crib[100] shall stand at the king's
        mess.[101] 'Tis a chuff;[102] but, as I say, spacious in the posses-
95   sion of dirt.
      OSRIC: Sweet lord, if your lordship were at leisure, I should
        impart a thing to you from his Majesty.
      HAMLET: I will receive it, sir, with all diligence of spirit. Put your
        bonnet to his right use. 'Tis for the head.
100   OSRIC: I thank your lordship, it is very hot.
      HAMLET: No, believe me, 'tis very cold; the wind is northerly.

[93]*thrust*
[94]*cruel*

[95]*election to the throne*
[96]*fishing line*
[97]*own*

[98]*finish*

[99]*insignificant person*

[100]*feed stall*
[101]*dining table*
[102]*chattering bird*

OSRIC: It is indifferent cold, my lord, indeed.

HAMLET: But yet methinks it is very sultry and hot for my complexion.

105 OSRIC: Exceedingly, my lord; it is very sultry, as 'twere—I cannot tell how. But, my lord, his Majesty bade me signify to you that he has laid a great wager on your head. Sir, this is the matter—

HAMLET: I beseech you remember—

[Hamlet moves him to put on his hat.]

110 OSRIC: Nay, good my lord; for mine ease, in good faith. Sir, here is newly come to court Laertes; believe me, an absolute gentleman, full of most excellent differences, of very soft[103] society and great showing. Indeed, to speak feelingly of him, he is the card[104] or calendar[105] of gentry; for you

115 shall find in him the continent of what part a gentleman would see.

HAMLET: Sir, his definement[106] suffers no perdition[107] in you; though, I know, to divide him inventorially[108] would dizzy the arithmetic of memory, and yet but yaw[109] neither, in

120 respect of his quick sail. But, in the verity[110] of extolment,[111] I take him to be a soul of great article,[112] and his infusion[113] of such dearth and rareness as, to make true diction[114] of him, his semblable[115] is his mirror, and who else would trace him, his umbrage,[116] nothing more.

125 OSRIC: Your lordship speaks most infallibly of him.

HAMLET: The concernancy,[117] sir? Why do we wrap the gentleman in our more rawer[118] breath?

OSRIC: Sir?

HORATIO: Is't not possible to understand in another tongue?

130 You will to't, sir, really.

HAMLET: What imports the nomination[119] of this gentleman?

OSRIC: Of Laertes?

HORATIO: *[Aside.]* His purse is empty already. All's golden words are spent.

135 HAMLET: Of him, sir.

OSRIC: I know you are not ignorant—

HAMLET: I would you did, sir; yet, in faith, if you did, it would not much approve[120] me. Well, sir?

OSRIC: You are not ignorant of what excellence Laertes is—

140 HAMLET: I dare not confess that, lest I should compare with

---

[103]*gentle*

[104]*map*

[105]*guide*

[106]*description (In the next lines, Hamlet speaks in exaggerated language, mocking Osric.)*

[107]*harm*

[108]*i.e., to make an ordered list of his good qualities*

[109]*miss the mark*

[110]*truth*

[111]*praise*

[112]*importance*

[113]*mixture*

[114]*description*

[115]*likeness*

[116]*shadow*

[117]*purpose*

[118]*crude*

[119]*mention*

[120]*compliment*

him in excellence; but to know a man well were to know himself.

OSRIC: I mean, sir, for his weapon; but in the imputation[121] laid on him by them, in his meed[122] he's unfellowed.[123]

145 HAMLET: What's his weapon?

OSRIC: Rapier and dagger.

HAMLET: That's two of his weapons. But, well.

OSRIC: The King, sir, hath wager'd with him six Barbary horses; against the which he has impawned,[124] as I take it, six French
150 rapiers and poniards,[125] with their assigns,[126] as girdle,[127] hanger,[128] and so. Three of the carriages, in faith, are very dear to fancy, very responsive[129] to the hilts, most delicate carriages, and of very liberal[130] conceit.[131]

HAMLET: What call you the carriages?

155 HORATIO: *[Aside to Hamlet.]* I knew you must be edified[132] by the margent[133] ere you had done.

OSRIC: The carriages, sir, are the hangers.

HAMLET: The phrase would be more German[134] to the matter if we could carry a cannon by our sides. I would it might
160 be hangers till then. But on! Six Barbary horses against six French swords, their assigns, and three liberal-conceited carriages—that's the French bet against the Danish. Why is this 'impawned,' as you call it?

OSRIC: The King, sir, hath laid,[135] sir, that, in a dozen passes
165 between yourself and him, he shall not exceed you three hits, he hath laid on twelve for nine, and it would come to imme-diate trial, if your lordship would vouchsafe the answer.[136]

HAMLET: How if I answer no?

OSRIC: I mean, my lord, the opposition of your person in trial.

170 HAMLET: Sir, I will walk here in the hall. If it please his Majesty, it is the breathing[137] time of day with me. Let the foils be brought, the gentleman willing, and the King hold his pur-pose, I will win for him an I can; if not, I will gain nothing but my shame and the odd[138] hits.

175 OSRIC: Shall I redeliver you e'en so?

HAMLET: To this effect,[139] sir, after what flourish[140] your nature will.

OSRIC: I commend my duty to your lordship.

HAMLET: Yours, yours. He does well to commend it himself;
180 there are no tongues else for's turn.

[121] *reputation*

[122] *worth*

[123] *unmatched*

[124] *wagered*

[125] *daggers*

[126] *accessories*

[127] *belts*

[128] *sword-straps*

[129] *matched*

[130] *noble*

[131] *design*

[132] *instructed*

[133] *margin notes*

[134] *relevant*

[135] *wagered*

[136] *i.e., answer the challenge by con-senting to duel*

[137] *exercise*

[138] *random*

[139] *meaning*

[140] *embellishment*

141*kind of bird said to grow up very quickly*

142*formally bow to*

143*mother's breast*

144*group*

145*worthless*

146*frothy*†

147*considered*

148*selected*

149*polite*

150*greeting*

151*misgiving*

152*arrival*

153*predictions about what will happen*

154*a reference to Matthew 10:29-31*

HORATIO: This lapwing[141] runs away with the shell on his head.†

HAMLET: He did comply[142] with his dug[143] before he sucked it. Thus has he—and many more of the same bevy[144] that I

185   know the drossy[145] age dotes on—only got the tune of the time and outward habit of encounter, a kind of yesty[146] collection, which carries them through and through the most fanned[147] and winnowed[148] opinions; and do but blow them to their trial, the bubbles are out.

Enter a Lord.

LORD: My lord, his Majesty commended him to you by young

190   Osric, who brings back to him that you attend him in the hall. He sends to know if your pleasure hold to play with Laertes, or that you will take longer time.

HAMLET: I am constant to my purposes; they follow the King's pleasure. If his fitness speaks, mine is ready; now or when-

195   soever, provided I be so able as now.

LORD: The King and Queen and all are coming down.

HAMLET: In happy time.

LORD: The Queen desires you to use some gentle[149] entertainment[150] to Laertes before you fall to play.

200   HAMLET: She well instructs me.

HORATIO: You will lose this wager, my lord.

HAMLET: I do not think so. Since he went into France I have been in continual practice. I shall win at the odds. But thou wouldst not think how ill all's here about my heart. But it

205   is no matter.

HORATIO: Nay, good my lord—

HAMLET: It is but foolery; but it is such a kind of gain-giving[151] as would perhaps trouble a woman.

HORATIO: If your mind dislike anything, obey it. I will forestall

210   their repair[152] hither and say you are not fit.

HAMLET: Not a whit. We defy augury;[153] there's a special providence† in the fall of a sparrow.[154] If it be now, 'tis not to come, if it be not to come, it will be now; if it be not now, yet it will come. The readiness is all. Since no man has

215   aught of what he leaves, what is't to leave betimes? Let be.

[Enter King, Queen, Laertes, Osric, and Lords, with other Attendants with foils and gauntlets. A table prepared with flagons of wine on it.]

KING: Come, Hamlet, come, and take this hand from me.
　　　　　[The King puts Laertes' hand into Hamlet's.]
HAMLET: Give me your pardon, sir. I have done you wrong;
　　　But pardon't, as you are a gentleman.
　　　This presence knows,
220　And you must needs have heard, how I am punish'd
　　　With sore distraction. What I have done
　　　That might your nature, honour, and exception
　　　Roughly awake, I here proclaim was madness.
　　　Was't Hamlet wrong'd Laertes? Never Hamlet.
225　If Hamlet from himself be taken away,
　　　And when he's not himself does wrong Laertes,
　　　Then Hamlet does it not, Hamlet denies it.
　　　Who does it, then? His madness. If't be so,
　　　Hamlet is of the faction[155] that is wrong'd;
230　His madness is poor Hamlet's enemy.
　　　Sir, in this audience,
　　　Let my disclaiming[156] from a purposed[157] evil
　　　Free me so far in your most generous thoughts
　　　That I have shot my arrow o'er the house
235　And hurt my brother.
LAERTES: I am satisfied in nature,
　　　Whose motive in this case should stir me most
　　　To my revenge. But in my terms of honour
　　　I stand aloof, and will no reconcilement
240　Till by some elder masters of known honour
　　　I have a voice and precedent[158] of peace
　　　To keep my name ungor'd.[159] But till that time
　　　I do receive your offer'd love like love,
　　　And will not wrong it.
245 HAMLET: I embrace it freely,
　　　And will this brother's wager frankly[160] play.—
　　　Give us the foils. Come on.
LAERTES: Come, one for me.
HAMLET: I'll be your foil, Laertes. In mine ignorance
250　Your skill shall, like a star i' the darkest night,
　　　Stick fiery off indeed.
LAERTES: You mock me, sir.
HAMLET: No, by this hand.
KING: Give them the foils, young Osric. Cousin Hamlet,
255　You know the wager?

[155]*party*

[156]*renouncing*

[157]*intended*

[158]*legal precedent*

[159]*unharmed*

[160]*freely*

HAMLET: Very well, my lord.

    Your Grace has laid the odds o' the weaker side.

KING: I do not fear it, I have seen you both;

161*considered better*

    But since he is better'd,[161] we have therefore odds.

260 LAERTES: This is too heavy; let me see another.

HAMLET: This likes me well. These foils have all a length?

OSRIC: Ay, my good lord.

                                 [They prepare to play.]

KING: Set me the stoups of wine upon that table.

    If Hamlet give the first or second hit,

265   Or quit in answer of the third exchange,

    Let all the battlements their ordnance fire;

    The King shall drink to Hamlet's better breath,

162*large pearl*

    And in the cup an union[162] shall he throw

    Richer than that which four successive kings

270   In Denmark's crown have worn. Give me the cups;

163*kettle drum*

    And let the kettle[163] to the trumpet speak,

    The trumpet to the cannoneer without,

    The cannons to the heavens, the heaven to earth,

    'Now the King drinks to Hamlet.' Come, begin.

275   And you the judges, bear a wary eye.

HAMLET: Come on, sir.

LAERTES: Come, my lord.

HAMLET: One.

LAERTES: No.

280 HAMLET: Judgment!

OSRIC: A hit, a very palpable hit.

LAERTES: Well, again!

KING: Stay, give me drink. Hamlet, this pearl is thine;

    Here's to thy health.

                   Drum, trumpets, and shots. A piece goes off.

285   Give him the cup.

HAMLET: I'll play this bout first; set it by awhile.

    Come. Another hit. What say you?

LAERTES: A touch, a touch; I do confess.

KING: Our son shall win.

290 QUEEN: He's fat, and scant of breath.

    Here, Hamlet, take my napkin, rub thy brows.

    The Queen carouses to thy fortune, Hamlet.

HAMLET: Good madam!

KING: Gertrude, do not drink.

295 QUEEN: I will, my lord; I pray you pardon me.

KING: It is the poison'd cup; it is too late.

HAMLET: I dare not drink yet, madam—by-and-by.

QUEEN: Come, let me wipe thy face.

LAERTES: My lord, I'll hit him now.

300 KING: I do not think't.

LAERTES: And yet it is almost against my conscience.

HAMLET: Come for the third, Laertes! You but dally.

I pray you, pass with your best violence;

I am afeard you make a wanton of me.

305 LAERTES: Say you so? Come on. Play.

OSRIC: Nothing, neither way.

LAERTES: Have at you now!

> [*Laertes wounds Hamlet. Then in scuffling, they*
> *change rapiers, and Hamlet wounds Laertes.*]

KING: Part them! They are incensed.

HAMLET: Nay come! again!

310 OSRIC: Look to the Queen there, ho!

HORATIO: They bleed on both sides. How is it, my lord?

OSRIC: How is't, Laertes?

LAERTES: Why, as a woodcock to mine own springe, Osric.

I am justly kill'd with mine own treachery.

315 HAMLET: How does the Queen?

KING: She swoons to see them bleed.

QUEEN: No, no! the drink, the drink!—O my dear Hamlet!—

The drink, the drink! I am poison'd.

HAMLET: O villainy! Ho! let the door be lock'd.

320   Treachery! Seek it out.

LAERTES: It is here, Hamlet. Hamlet, thou art slain;

No medicine in the world can do thee good.

In thee there is not half an hour of life.

The treacherous instrument is in thy hand,

325   Unbated and envenom'd. The foul practice

Hath turn'd itself on me. Lo, here I lie,

Never to rise again. Thy mother's poison'd.

I can no more. The King, the King's to blame.

HAMLET: The point envenom'd too! Then, venom, to thy work.

> [*Stabs the King.*]

330 ALL: Treason! treason!

KING: O, yet defend me, friends! I am but hurt.

HAMLET: Here, thou incestuous, murderous, damned Dane,
 Drink off this potion! Is thy union here?
 Follow my mother.   *[King dies.]*

335 LAERTES: He is justly served.
 It is a poison temper'd by himself.
 Exchange forgiveness with me, noble Hamlet.
 Mine and my father's death come not upon thee,
 Nor thine on me!   *[Dies.]*

340 HAMLET: Heaven make thee free of it! I follow thee.
 I am dead, Horatio. Wretched Queen, adieu!
 You that look pale and tremble at this chance,
 That are but mutes or audience to this act,
 Had I but time—as this fell sergeant, Death,

345 Is strict in his arrest—O, I could tell you—
 But let it be. Horatio, I am dead;
 Thou livest; report me and my cause aright
 To the unsatisfied.

HORATIO: Never believe it.

164*ancient* 350 I am more an antique[164] Roman† than a Dane.
 Here's yet some liquor left.

HAMLET: As th'art a man,
 Give me the cup. Let go! By heaven, I'll have't.
 O God, Horatio, what a wounded name,

355 Things standing thus unknown, shall live behind me!
 If thou didst ever hold me in thy heart,

165*pleasure* Absent thee from felicity[165] awhile,
 And in this harsh world draw thy breath in pain,
 To tell my story.

       [March far off, and shot within.]

360 What warlike noise is this?

OSRIC: Young Fortinbras, with conquest come from Poland,
 To the ambassadors of England gives

166*greeting shot* This warlike volley.[166]

HAMLET: O, I die, Horatio!

167*overcomes* 365 The potent poison quite o'er-crows[167] my spirit.
 I cannot live to hear the news from England,
 But I do prophesy the election lights[168]

168*lands* On Fortinbras. He has my dying voice.

So tell him, with the occurrents,[169] more and less,
370   Which have solicited[170]—The rest is silence.   *[Dies.]*
HORATIO: Now cracks a noble heart. Good night, sweet prince,
And flights of angels sing thee to thy rest!   *[March within.]*
Why does the drum come hither?

Enter Fortinbras and the Ambassadors, [with Drum, Colours, and Attendants.]

FORTINBRAS: Where is this sight?
375 HORATIO: What is it you will see?
If aught of woe or wonder, cease your search.
FORTINBRAS: This quarry[171] cries[172] on havoc.[173] O proud Death,
What feast is toward[174] in thine eternal cell
That thou so many princes at a shot
380   So bloodily hast struck?
AMBASSADOR: The sight is dismal;
And our affairs from England come too late.
The ears are senseless that should give us hearing
To tell him his commandment is fulfill'd
385   That Rosencrantz and Guildenstern are dead.
Where should we have our thanks?
HORATIO: Not from his mouth,
Had it the ability of life to thank you.
He never gave commandment for their death.
390   But since, so jump upon this bloody question,
You from the Polack wars, and you from England,
Are here arrived, give order that these bodies
High on a stage be placed to the view;
And let me speak to the yet unknowing world
395   How these things came about. So shall you hear
Of carnal, bloody and unnatural acts;
Of accidental judgments, casual slaughters;
Of deaths put on by cunning and forced cause;
And, in this upshot, purposes mistook
400   Fall'n on the inventors'[175] heads. All this can I
Truly deliver.
FORTINBRAS: Let us haste to hear it,
And call the noblest to the audience.

---

[169]*occurrences*

[170]*brought about*

[171]*pile of corpses*

[172]*proclaims, shows*

[173]*unlimited slaughter*†

[174]*about to happen*

[175]*those who devised the plan*

       For me, with sorrow I embrace my fortune.
405   I have some rights of memory in this kingdom,
       Which now, to claim my vantage doth invite me.
    HORATIO: Of that I shall have also cause to speak,
       And from his mouth whose voice will draw on more.
       But let this same be presently perform'd,
410   Even while men's minds are wild, lest more mischance
       On plots and errors happen.
   FORTINBRAS: Let four captains
       Bear Hamlet like a soldier to the stage;
       For he was likely, had he been put on,
415   To have proved most royal; and, for his passage,
      The soldiers' music and the rites of war
       Speak loudly for him.
       Take up the bodies. Such a sight as this
       Becomes the field, but here shows much amiss.
420   Go, bid the soldiers shoot.

Exeunt [marching; after the which a peal of ordnance is shot off.]

FINIS

❧

VOCABULARY AND GLOSSARY

Act I, Scene I

Fortinbras – At the time the ghost appears, the Danes are in the middle of an on-and-off war with Norway. Prince Hamlet's father, King Hamlet, previously defeated and killed King Fortinbras of Norway; by legal contract, the Norwegian lands mentioned in the contract then became property of Denmark. Now the Norwegian king's son, also named Fortinbras, is claiming that the lands were stolen and preparing to wage war on Denmark to regain them.

the mightiest Julius – Julius Caesar, the Roman dictator assassinated in 44 BC; in Shakespeare's *Julius Caesar*, the supernatural events that surround Caesar's death (shooting stars, ghosts, unusual animals) are described in detail.

Act I, Scene II

Wittenberg – a German city famous for its university; Martin Luther started the Protestant Reformation in Wittenberg in 1517. Some critics have identified Hamlet with Martin Luther.

Hyperion – in Greek mythology, the original god of the sun (this power was later transferred to Apollo)

satyr – a mythological creature that is half-man, half-goat; satyrs were supposed to be crude and hypersexual.

Niobe – in Greek mythology, the woman whose children were killed after she boasted about them; she was turned to stone, but continued to weep.

Hercules – in Greek and Roman mythology, the strongest man in the world, forced to do twelve difficult labors

Act I, Scene III

tenders – Polonius plays on the word several times. He is given to somewhat clumsy wordplay; it contributes to the impression of him as long-winded and pompous.

parley – a formal talk between two warring parties; Polonius, in his mixed-up way, means that Ophelia should not stake her *entreatments* (formal negotiations for surrender) on a simple conversation.

Act I, Scene IV

evil – Some texts have *eale* (another word for *yeast*) instead of *evil*. This reading implies that even a small fault can, like yeast does bread, change a whole human being or country. Note the use of the word *o'erleavens*, meaning "makes bread rise too much," earlier in the passage.

canonized – in this context, "given Christian burial"; canonization usually refers to the process by which, after death, someone becomes a saint.

Nemean lion – in Greek mythology, a lion so strong that no weapons could kill it; Hercules, as one of his twelve labors, strangled it with his bare hands.

Act I, Scene V

Lethe – in Greek mythology, the river of forgetfulness that runs through the underworld

quicksilver – another name for mercury, an element that moves quickly and unpredictably

unhouseled, unanaled – without the Holy Sacrament (the bread and wine consumed by Catholics as part of Holy Communion) and without Last Rites (the prayers said for the dying); Hamlet's father was murdered before he had the chance to be absolved of his sins.

Act II, Scene I

windlasses – literally, roundabout trips made to surround a hunted animal

bias – a curve in a bowling alley that leads the ball to a desired spot

Act II, Scene II

quintessence – In medieval philosophy, *quintessence* was the fifth element (after fire, water, earth, and air). It was a mysterious, invisible, divine substance present in all things. When Hamlet calls mankind the "quintessence of dust," he is saying that human beings, for all their heavenly design, seem to be no more than dirt.

sere – the trigger of a gun; something "tickle o' the sere" (like the lungs of someone ready to laugh) is easily triggered.

blank verse – unrhymed iambic pentameter (having five *feet*, or units of rhythm, which are generally made up of an unstressed syllable followed by a stressed syllable). See *Strategies for Understanding Shakespeare's Language* on page 4.

tragedians of the city – The practice of replacing accomplished adult actors with children (who drew crowds because of their cuteness) had recently gained popularity. The players are probably expressing the views of Shakespeare's own company.

Hercules and his load too – The Globe Theatre, home of Shakespeare's acting troupe, had a sign depicting Hercules holding up the world.

tragedy, comedy, history, pastoral – different types of plays; *pastoral* plays are set in the country and usually feature shepherds or rustic characters.

Seneca – Lucius Seneca (c. 4 BC-AD 65), a Roman dramatist highly influential upon Renaissance tragic playwrights

Plautus – (254 BC-184 BC), a Roman writer of comic plays; Shakespeare's early comedies are based on popular Italian farces, which often took their plot from Plautus' plays.

Jephthah – in the Bible (Judges XI), a judge who promises to sacrifice his virgin daughter in return for military victory; Hamlet sings a popular ballad based on the story.

beard – to defy; also a reference to the beard now worn by the player, who once played women's roles, but has been pushed out of them by the child players.

Æneas' tale to Dido – In the Roman poet Virgil's epic poem *The Æneid*, Æneas, the last surviving Trojan of the Trojan War, wins the love of Dido, queen of Carthage, by telling her stories of the war.

Pyrrhus – a son of Achilles, whose cruel murder of the elderly Trojan King Priam is graphically described in *Æneid*

ominous horse – According to the *Æneid*, the Greeks managed to enter the city of Troy by presenting a huge wooden horse as a gift to the Trojans. The horse was actually hollow and filled with Greek soldiers, who emerged at night and sacked the city.

gules – a term used in *heraldry* (a system by which coats of arms and genealogies are organized) meaning "red"

Cyclops – one-eyed giants who worked in Vulcan's forge making armor for the gods

Act III, Scene I

inoculate – another word for *graft*, meaning "to transfer a cutting from one plant onto another plant"; the *stock* of the new plant then becomes part of its host. Hamlet is saying that even if virtue is added to his nature, he will retain some of his old wickedness.

Act III, Scene II

groundlings – Theater audiences in Shakespeare's time were divided between the groundlings (poorer people who paid a penny for admission and stood in the open area before the stage) and wealthier patrons, who sat in a raised balcony area (called "Heaven").

Termagant – In medieval plays, Termagant was a Muslim god who was usually over-acted (that is, played as noisy and violent).

Herod – the king of the Jews at the time of Jesus' death; in medieval plays, he is portrayed as a raging tyrant.

Vulcan's stithy – Vulcan was the Roman god of metalworking and fire; his *stithy* is the forge where he made the armor of the gods.

hobby-horse – a stick horse ridden in the May Day celebration; also another word for "whore."

Hecate – the Greek goddess of witchcraft and black magic (sometimes associated with Diana, goddess of the hunt and the moon)

purgation – medicine in Shakespeare's time relied on the theory of *humors*. This theory stated that the body was controlled by four fluids:

- choler, or yellow bile, which caused irritability, or choleric qualities
- black bile, which made a person *melancholy*, or sad
- blood, which made a person *sanguine*, or cheerful
- phlegm, which caused a phlegmatic (sluggish and dull) mood

When these fluids were imbalanced, a person became sick or went insane. Hamlet says that if he put Claudius to *purgation* (bodily or spiritual cleansing), Claudius would just become more choleric.

Act III, Scene III

primal eldest curse – Claudius makes reference to the story of Cain and Abel (Genesis 4:1-17), in which Cain, the oldest brother, kills Abel out of jealousy.

hent – i.e., may you know a worse time for Claudius to die

Act III, Scene IV – Act IV, Scene IV

—

Act IV, Scene V

cockle hat – Ophelia sings a popular song about a pilgrim who has been to the shrine of St. James of Compostela (as evidenced by the *cockle*, or seashell, on his hat).

counter – literally, going the wrong way on a hunting trail

Act IV, Scene VI – Act IV, Scene VII

—

Act V, Scene I

goodman delver – "Goodman" is a title or form of address for a man of the working class.

by the card – a compass-card used by sailors and marked exactly with navigation points

old Pelion – a mountain which, according to Greek mythology, the Titans tried to pile upon several other mountains (Ossa and Olympus) in order to reach the gods

Act V, Scene II

yeoman's – In feudal society, a *yeoman* was ranked lower than a lord; *yeoman's service* is faithful, dependable service, such as might be provided to a lord.

changeling – a fairy child left in place of a human infant kidnapped by fairies; Hamlet uses the word to mean "substitution."

Popp'd in between the election and my hopes – This seems to indicate that the Danish king was elected instead of given the throne by birthright.

with his shell on his head – Horatio makes fun of Osric's hurry to do everything; he calls Osric a *lapwing* (a bird thought to grow to adulthood very quickly) and adds to the picture by saying that Osric is running off right after "hatching," with his shell on his head. Hamlet then says that Osric probably bowed to his own mother's breast.

yesty – Here, the image comes from baking; men like Osric, carried by their yeast-like reputations, pass the test of both foolish ("fond") and thoughtful ("winnowed") opinions, but careful examination ("do but blow on them") shows that they are worthless ("the bubbles are out").

special providence – a reference to Matthew 10:29-31, in which Jesus asks, "Are not two sparrows sold for a farthing? and one of them shall not fall on the ground without your Father. But the very hairs of your head are all numbered. Fear ye not therefore, ye are of more value than many sparrows."

antique Roman – The Stoics were followers of a philosophy started in Greece around 300 BC. The core principle of Stoicism was acceptance of one's lack of control over external circumstances. Later Romans took the philosophy and made it their own, turning its focus to strong morality and bravery in the face of death. A good Stoic would commit suicide before he compromised himself. Horatio makes known his intent to follow this "antique Roman" ideal and commit suicide.

cries on havoc – Fortinbras says that his "quarry" (a hunting term meaning "a pile of carcasses") is evidence that someone "cried havoc"—gave the signal for unlimited slaughter.

Insightful and Reader-Friendly, Yet Affordable

Prestwick House Literary Touchstone Classic Editions–
The Editions By Which All Others May Be Judged

Every *Prestwick House Literary Touchstone Classic* is enhanced with Reading Pointers for Sharper Insight to improve comprehension and provide insights that will help students recognize key themes, symbols, and plot complexities. In addition, each title includes a Glossary of the more difficult words and concepts.

For the Shakespeare titles, along with the Reading Pointers and Glossary, we include margin notes and various strategies to understanding the language of Shakespeare.

New titles are constantly being added; call or visit our website for current listing.

Special Educator's Discount – At Least
50% Off

		Retail Price	Educator's Discount
200053	Adventures of Huckleberry Finn	$4.99	**$2.49**
202118	Antigone	$3.99	**$1.99**
200141	Awakening, The	$5.99	**$2.99**
200179	Christmas Carol, A	$3.99	**$1.99**
200694	Doll's House, A	$3.99	**$1.99**
200054	Frankenstein	$4.99	**$1.99**
200091	Hamlet	$3.99	**$1.99**
200074	Heart of Darkness	$3.99	**$1.99**
200147	Importance of Being Earnest, The	$3.99	**$1.99**
200146	Julius Caesar	$3.99	**$1.99**
200125	Macbeth	$3.99	**$1.99**
200081	Midsummer Night's Dream, A	$3.99	**$1.99**
200079	Narrative of the Life of Frederick Douglass	$3.99	**$1.99**
200564	Oedipus Rex	$3.99	**$1.99**
200095	Othello	$3.99	**$1.99**
200193	Romeo and Juliet	$3.99	**$0.99**
200132	Scarlet Letter, The	$5.99	**$2.99**
200251	Tale of Two Cities, A	$6.99	**$3.49**

PH Prestwick House Prestwick House, Inc. • P.O. Box 658, Clayton, DE 19938
Phone (800) 932-4593 • Fax (888) 718-9333 • www.prestwickhouse.com